perfect
vegetarian

Bath · New York · Singapore · Hong Kong · Cologne · Delhi · Melbourne

This edition published by Parragon in 2008

Parragon Publishing
Queen Street House
4 Queen Street
Bath BA1 1HE, UK

ISBN 978-1-4075-2624-9

Printed in Indonesia

This book uses imperial, metric, and US cup measurements. Follow the same units of measurement throughout; do not mix imperial and metric. All spoon measurements are level, unless otherwise stated: teaspoons are assumed to be 5ml, and tablespoons are assumed to be 15ml. Unless otherwise stated, milk is assumed to be whole, eggs and individual fruits such as bananas are medium, and pepper is freshly ground black pepper.

Recipes using raw or very lightly cooked eggs should be avoided by infants, the elderly, pregnant women, convalescents, and anyone suffering from an illness. Pregnant and breast-feeding women are advised to avoid eating peanuts and peanut products.

Vegetable Assortment in the Kitchen © Hussenot/photocuisine/Corbis.

perfect
vegetarian

introduction

Following a vegetarian diet was once considered to be rather eccentric and certainly very dull! However, in recent years more and more people have chosen to embrace a meat-free diet, for a number of reasons. The most obvious of these is a desire not to eat animals or fish, but health issues often come into the equation, too—for example, sufferers of irritable bowel syndrome often find that meat is one of the triggers for the symptoms. Meat and fish can also be expensive, so even non-vegetarians often choose to have two or three meat-free meals each week.

The really good news is that the ever-increasing interest in

vegetarianism has raised its profile in the world of gastronomy. Chefs have risen to the challenge with skill and enthusiasm and have come up with some truly creative recipes—and the meat-free diet is no longer dull!

If you are new to vegetarianism, it is important to remember that you cannot simply exclude meat and fish from your usual recipes, because this will deprive you of protein and other vital nutrients that are essential to your  health and wellbeing. Meat and fish must be replaced with other protein- and nutrient-rich foods such as beans, nuts and seeds, bean curd, and dairy products. If you have allergies to any of these foods, take advice from your doctor or a nutritionist to ensure that you will not damage your health instead of enhancing it.

Whether you are planning to be a 'proper' vegetarian, or you are having vegetarian guests to dinner, or you just want to ring the changes and have an occasional meal without meat, there are  some fabulous ideas in this book, taken from around the world. For the best results, choose really fresh, top-quality ingredients—this will ensure that you get the maximum goodness out of your food, as well as superb flavor.

Have fun experimenting!

light bites & appetizers

Many of the world's favorite classic dishes are made with vegetables and there are some great recipes here for soups, dips, and appetizers. Try a light and delicate Watercress Soup, a hearty White Bean Soup, or the thick and satisfying Monk's Soup—there's no hint of austerity here, whatever the name might imply! Put together a Spanish tapas selection, such as Salted Almonds, Cracked Marinated Olives, Eggplant Dip, Sautéed Garlic Mushrooms, and Figs with Bleu Cheese, or do as the French do and start your meal with the Mixed Salad Selection—a refreshing combination of celery root, carrot, and beet that will really make your palate tingle.

Some of these recipes also make ideal light dishes. For brunch, lunch, or a late-evening snack, try Zucchini Fritters with Yogurt Dip, Cheese & Herb Soufflés with Sautéed Mushrooms, Sweet Potato, Mint, and Feta Patties, or Stuffed Portabello Mushrooms. If you love Mexican-style food, go for Guacamole or Black Bean Nachos, and for a hint of the Middle East try Hummus Dip or Falafel with Tahini Sauce. There is enough nutrition in these dishes to keep you feeling satisfied for hours!

If, however, you just want the most perfect, simple, elegant appetizer, serve Asparagus with Melted Butter. Wonderful!

salted almonds

ingredients

SERVES 6–8

8 oz/225 g/scant 1^1/$_2$ cups
   whole almonds, in their
   skins or blanched
   (see method)
4 tbsp Spanish olive oil
coarse sea salt
1 tsp paprika or ground
   cumin (optional)

method

1 Fresh almonds in their skins are superior in taste, but blanched almonds are much more convenient. If the almonds are not blanched, put them in a bowl, cover with boiling water for 3–4 minutes, then plunge them into cold water for 1 minute. Drain them well in a strainer, then slide off the skins between your fingers. Dry the almonds well on paper towels.

2 Put the olive oil in a roasting pan and swirl it round so that it covers the bottom. Add the almonds and toss them in the pan so that they are evenly coated in the oil, then spread them out in a single layer.

3 Roast the almonds in a preheated oven, 350°F/180°C, for 20 minutes, or until they are light golden brown, tossing several times during the cooking. Drain the almonds on paper towels, then transfer them to a bowl.

4 While the almonds are still warm, sprinkle with plenty of sea salt and the paprika or cumin, if using, and toss well together to coat. Serve the almonds warm or cold. The almonds are at their best when served freshly cooked, so, if possible, cook them on the day that you plan to eat them. However, they can be stored in an airtight container for up to 3 days.

cracked marinated olives

ingredients

SERVES 8

1 lb/450 g can or jar unpitted
   large green olives, drained
4 garlic cloves, peeled
2 tsp coriander seeds
1 small lemon
4 sprigs of fresh thyme
4 feathery stalks of fennel
2 small fresh red chiles
   (optional)
pepper
Spanish extra-virgin olive oil,
   to cover

method

1 To allow the flavors of the marinade to penetrate the olives, place the olives on a cutting board and, using a rolling pin, bash them lightly so that they crack slightly. Alternatively, use a sharp knife to cut a lengthwise slit in each olive as far as the pit. Using the flat side of a broad knife, lightly crush each garlic clove. Using a mortar and pestle, crack the coriander seeds. Cut the lemon, with its rind, into small chunks.

2 Put the olives, garlic, coriander seeds, lemon chunks, thyme sprigs, fennel, and chiles, if using, in a large bowl and toss together. Season with pepper, but you should not need to add salt as preserved olives are usually salty enough. Pack the ingredients tightly into a glass jar with a lid. Pour in enough olive oil to cover the olives, then seal the jar tightly.

3 Let the olives stand at room temperature for 24 hours, then marinate in the refrigerator for at least 1 week but preferably 2 weeks before serving. From time to time, gently give the jar a shake to remix the ingredients. Return the olives to room temperature and remove from the oil to serve. Provide toothpicks for spearing the olives.

guacamole

ingredients

SERVES 4

2 large, ripe avocados

juice of 1 lime, or to taste

2 tsp olive oil

$1/2$ onion, finely chopped

1 fresh green chile, such as
poblano, seeded and
finely chopped

1 garlic clove, crushed

$1/4$ tsp ground cumin

1 tbsp chopped fresh cilantro,
plus extra leaves to
garnish (optional)

salt and pepper

method

1 Cut the avocados in half lengthwise and twist the 2 halves in opposite directions to separate. Stab the pit with the point of a sharp knife and lift out.

2 Peel, then coarsely chop, the avocado halves and place in a nonmetallic bowl. Squeeze over the lime juice and add the oil.

3 Mash the avocados with a fork until the desired consistency is reached—either chunky or smooth. Blend in the onion, chile, garlic, cumin, and chopped cilantro, then season with salt and pepper.

4 Transfer to a serving dish and serve at once, to avoid discoloration, garnished with the cilantro leaves, if liked.

eggplant dip

ingredients

SERVES 6–8

olive oil

1 large eggplant,
   about 14 oz/400 g

2 scallions, chopped finely

1 large garlic clove, crushed

2 tbsp finely chopped fresh
   parsley

salt and pepper

smoked sweet Spanish paprika,
   to garnish

French bread, to serve

method

1 Heat 4 tablespoons of oil in a large skillet over medium-high heat. Add the eggplant slices and cook on both sides until soft and starting to brown. Remove from the skillet and set aside to cool. The slices will release the oil again as they cool.

2 Heat another tablespoon of oil in the skillet. Add the scallions and garlic and cook for 3 minutes, or until the scallions become soft. Remove from the heat and set aside with the eggplant slices to cool.

3 Transfer all the ingredients to a food processor and process just until a coarse purée forms. Transfer to a serving bowl and stir in the parsley. Taste and adjust the seasoning, if necessary. Serve at once, or cover and let chill until 15 minutes before required. Sprinkle with paprika and serve with slices of French bread.

hummus dip

ingredients

SERVES 8

8 oz/225 g/1^{1}/$_{3}$ cups dried
  chickpeas, covered with
  water and soaked
  overnight
juice of 2 large lemons
5 fl oz/150 ml/^{2}/$_{3}$ cup sesame
  seed paste
2 garlic cloves, crushed
4 tbsp extra-virgin olive oil
small pinch of ground cumin
salt and pepper
1 tsp paprika
chopped flat-leaf parsley,
  to garnish
pita bread, to serve

method

1 Drain the chickpeas, put in a pan, and cover with cold water. Bring to a boil then let simmer for about 2 hours, until very tender.

2 Drain the chickpeas, reserving a little of the liquid, and put in a food processor, reserving a few to garnish. Blend the chickpeas until smooth, gradually adding the lemon juice and enough reserved liquid to form a smooth, thick purée.

3 Add the sesame seed paste, garlic, 3 tablespoons of the olive oil, and the cumin and blend until smooth. Season with salt and pepper.

4 Turn the mixture into a shallow serving dish and chill in the refrigerator for 2–3 hours before serving.

5 To serve, mix the reserved olive oil with the paprika and drizzle over the top of the dish. Sprinkle with the parsley and the reserved chickpeas. Accompany with warm pita bread.

vegetable soup with pesto

ingredients

SERVES 4

32 fl oz/1 liter/4 cups
   fresh cold water
bouquet garni of 1 fresh parsley
   sprig, 1 fresh thyme sprig,
   and 1 bay leaf, tied together
   with clean string
2 celery stalks, chopped
3 baby leeks, chopped
4 baby carrots, chopped
5^{1}/$_{2}$ oz/150 g new potatoes,
   scrubbed and cut into
   bite-size chunks
4 tbsp shelled fava beans
   or peas
6 oz/175 g canned cannellini
   or flageolet beans, drained
   and rinsed
3 heads bok choy
5^{1}/$_{2}$ oz/150 g/generous
   3^{1}/$_{4}$ cups arugula
pepper

pesto

2 large handfuls fresh basil
   leaves
1 fresh green chile, seeded
2 garlic cloves
4 tbsp olive oil
1 tsp Parmesan cheese,
   finely grated

method

1 Put the water and bouquet garni into a large pan and add the celery, leeks, carrots, and potatoes. Bring to a boil, then reduce the heat and let simmer for 10 minutes.

2 Stir in the fava beans or peas and canned beans and let simmer for an additional 10 minutes. Stir in the bok choy and arugula, season with pepper and let simmer for an additional 2–3 minutes. Remove and discard the bouquet garni.

3 Meanwhile, to make the pesto, put the basil, chile, garlic, and oil into a food processor and pulse to form a thick paste. Stir in the cheese.

4 Stir most of the pesto into the soup, then ladle into warmed bowls. Top with the remaining pesto and serve at once.

white bean soup

ingredients

SERVES 4

6 oz/175 g/³/4 cup dried
   cannellini beans, soaked
   in cold water to cover
   overnight

48 fl oz/1.5 liters/6 cups
   vegetable stock

4 oz/115 g dried corallini,
   conchigliette piccole,
   or other soup pasta

6 tbsp olive oil

2 garlic cloves, finely chopped

4 tbsp chopped fresh
   flat-leaf parsley

salt and pepper

fresh crusty bread, to serve

method

1 Drain the soaked beans and place them in a large, heavy-bottom pan. Add the stock and bring to a boil. Partially cover the pan, then reduce the heat, and let simmer for 2 hours, or until tender.

2 Transfer about half the beans and a little of the stock to a food processor or blender and process to a smooth purée. Return the purée to the pan and stir well to mix. Return the soup to a boil.

3 Add the pasta to the soup, return to a boil, and cook for 10 minutes, or until tender.

4 Meanwhile, heat 4 tablespoons of the olive oil in a small pan. Add the garlic and cook over low heat, stirring frequently, for 4–5 minutes, or until golden. Stir the garlic into the soup and add the parsley. Season with salt and pepper and ladle into warmed soup bowls. Drizzle with the remaining olive oil and serve immediately with crusty bread.

watercress soup

ingredients

SERVES 4

2 bunches of watercress
(approx 7 oz/200 g),
thoroughly cleaned

3 tbsp butter

2 onions, chopped

8 oz/225 g potatoes, peeled
and roughly chopped

40 fl oz/1.25 liters/5 cups
vegetable stock or water

salt and pepper

whole nutmeg, for grating
(optional)

4 fl oz/125 ml/$^1/_2$ cup
crème fraîche, yogurt,
or sour cream

method

1 Remove the leaves from the stalks of the watercress and keep on one side. Roughly chop the stalks.

2 Melt the butter in a large pan over medium heat, add the onion, and cook for 4–5 minutes until soft. Do not brown.

3 Add the potato to the pan and mix well with the onion. Add the watercress stalks and the stock. Bring to a boil, then reduce the heat, cover, and simmer for 15–20 minutes until the potato is soft.

4 Add the watercress leaves and stir in to heat through. Remove from the heat and use a hand-held stick blender to process the soup until smooth. Alternatively, pour the soup into a blender, process until smooth, and return to the rinsed-out pan. Reheat and season with salt and pepper, adding a good grating of nutmeg, if using.

5 Serve in warm bowls with the crème fraîche spooned on top.

borscht

ingredients

SERVES 6

1 onion

4 tbsp butter

12 oz/350 g raw beet, cut into thin sticks, and 1 raw beet, grated

1 carrot, cut into thin sticks

3 celery stalks, thinly sliced

2 tomatoes, peeled, seeded, and chopped

2 large fresh dill sprigs

48 fl oz/1.5 liters/6 cups vegetable stock

1 tbsp white wine vinegar

1 tbsp sugar

salt and pepper

4 oz/115 g white cabbage, shredded

5 fl oz/150 ml/^{2}/$_3$ cup sour cream, to garnish

method

1 Slice the onion into rings. Melt the butter in a large, heavy-bottom pan over low heat. Add the onion and cook, stirring frequently, for 5 minutes or until softened. Add the beet sticks, carrot, celery, and tomatoes and cook, stirring frequently, for 4–5 minutes.

2 Snip one of the dill sprigs. Add the stock, vinegar, sugar, and the snipped dill to the pan. Season with salt and pepper. Bring to a boil, then reduce the heat and let simmer for 35–40 minutes until the vegetables are tender.

3 Stir in the cabbage, cover, and let simmer for an additional 10 minutes. Stir in the grated beet, with any juices, and cook for an additional 10 minutes. Ladle into warmed bowls. Garnish with a spoonful of sour cream and snip the remaining dill over the top.

monk's soup

ingredients

SERVES 4

32 fl oz/1 liter/4 cups
    vegetable stock
1 stalk lemongrass, center
    part only, finely chopped
1 tsp tamarind paste
pinch of dried red pepper
    flakes, or to taste
5 oz/140 g thin green beans,
    cut into 1-inch/2.5-cm
    pieces
1 tbsp light soy sauce
1 tsp brown sugar
juice of $1/2$ lime
9 oz/250 g firm bean curd,
    drained and cut into small
    cubes
2 scallions, sliced diagonally
2 oz/55 g enoki mushrooms,
    hard end of the stalks cut off
14 oz/400 g fresh udon noodles
    or thick Chinese egg
    noodles

method

1 Put the stock in a large pan with the lemongrass, tamarind paste, and red pepper flakes and bring to a boil, stirring until the tamarind dissolves. Lower the heat, add the green beans, and let simmer for 6 minutes. Add the soy sauce, brown sugar, and lime juice. Taste and stir in more sugar, lime juice, or red pepper flakes if liked.

2 Stir in the bean curd and scallions and continue simmering for just 1–2 minutes longer, or until the green beans are tender, but still with a bit of bite, and the bean curd is warm. Add the enoki mushrooms.

3 Pour boiling water over the udon noodles to separate them, then divide them among 4 large bowls and divide the soup among the bowls. The heat of the soup will warm the noodles.

chinese mushroom soup

ingredients

SERVES 4

$^1/_2$ oz/15 g dried Chinese
   wood ear mushrooms

4 oz/115 g dried thin Chinese
   egg noodles

2 tsp arrowroot or cornstarch

32 fl oz/1 liter/4 cups
   vegetable stock

2-inch/5-cm piece fresh
   gingerroot, peeled and
   sliced

2 tbsp dark soy sauce

2 tsp mirin or sweet sherry

1 tsp rice vinegar

4 small bok choy, each cut
   in half

salt and pepper

snipped fresh Chinese or
   ordinary chives, to garnish

method

1 Put the dried wood ear mushrooms in a heatproof bowl and pour over enough boiling water to cover, then let stand for 20 minutes, or until tender. Meanwhile, boil the noodles for 3 minutes, or according to the package instructions, until soft. Drain well and rinse with cold water to stop the noodles cooking, and set aside.

2 Strain the mushrooms through a strainer lined with a dish towel and reserve the liquid. Leave the mushrooms whole or slice them, depending on how large they are. Put the arrowroot in a wok or large pan and gradually stir in the reserved mushroom liquid. Add the vegetable stock, sliced gingerroot, soy sauce, mirin, rice vinegar, mushrooms, and bok choy and bring to a boil, stirring constantly. Lower the heat and let simmer for 15 minutes.

3 Add salt and pepper, but remember that soy sauce is salty so you might not need any salt at all—taste first. Use a slotted spoon to remove the pieces of gingerroot.

4 Divide the noodles among 4 bowls, then spoon the soup over and garnish with chives.

sautéed garlic mushrooms

ingredients

SERVES 6

1 lb/450 g white mushrooms
5 tbsp Spanish olive oil
2 garlic cloves, finely chopped
squeeze of lemon juice
salt and pepper
4 tbsp chopped fresh
    flat-leaf parsley
crusty bread, to serve

method

1 Wipe or brush clean the mushrooms, then trim off the stalks close to the caps. Cut any large mushrooms in half or into fourths. Heat the olive oil in a large, heavy-bottom skillet, add the garlic and cook for 30 seconds–1 minute, or until lightly browned. Add the mushrooms and sauté over high heat, stirring most of the time, until the mushrooms have absorbed all the oil in the skillet.

2 Reduce the heat to low. When the juices have come out of the mushrooms, increase the heat again, and sauté for 4–5 minutes, stirring most of the time, until the juices have almost evaporated. Add a squeeze of lemon juice and season with salt and pepper. Stir in the chopped parsley and cook for an additional minute.

3 Transfer the sautéed mushrooms to a warmed serving dish and serve piping hot or warm. Accompany with chunks or slices of crusty bread for mopping up the garlic cooking juices.

mixed salad selection

ingredients

SERVES 4–6

celery root rémoulade

1 large egg yolk

1 tbsp Dijon mustard

$^1/_2$ tsp red wine vinegar

5 fl oz/150 ml sunflower oil

salt and pepper

$1^1/_2$ tsp lemon juice

1 tsp salt

1 lb/450 g celery root

carrot salad

1 lb/450 g carrots, peeled

2 tbsp olive oil

2 tbsp freshly squeezed
    orange juice

salt and pepper

2 tbsp finely chopped
    almonds

1 tbsp finely chopped fresh
    flat-leaf parsley

beet salad

14 oz/400 g cooked beet,
    peeled

2 tbsp vinaigrette

1 tbsp snipped fresh chives

slices of French bread and
    unsalted butter, to serve

method

1 To make the rémoulade sauce, whiz the egg yolk, mustard, and red wine vinegar in a food processor or blender until blended. With the motor still running, pour the oil through the feed tube, drop by drop, until the sauce starts to thicken, then add the remainder of the oil in a slow, steady stream. Season with salt and pepper.

2 Put the lemon juice and salt in a large bowl of water. Finely shred the celery root into the acidulated water to prevent discoloration. Drain and pat dry, then stir into the rémoulade sauce. Let stand for 20 minutes at room temperature before serving.

3 To make the carrot salad, finely shred the carrots into a bowl with the olive oil and orange juice and toss together. Season with salt and pepper and cover and chill until required. Stir in the almonds and parsley just before serving.

4 To make the beet salad, cut the beet into $^1/_4$-inch/5-mm dice. Put the diced beet in a bowl, then add the vinaigrette and toss together. Cover and chill until required. Stir in the chives just before serving.

5 To serve, divide the celery root rémoulade, carrot salad, and beet salad among individual plates and accompany with plenty of French bread and butter.

figs with bleu cheese

ingredients

SERVES 6

caramelized
almonds

100 g/3^1/$_2$ oz/^{1}/$_2$ cup
    superfine sugar
4 oz/115 g/generous ^{3}/$_4$ cup
    whole almonds, blanched
    or unblanched

12 ripe figs
12 oz/350 g Spanish bleu
    cheese, such as Picós,
    crumbled
extra-virgin olive oil

method

1 First make the caramelized almonds. Put the sugar in a pan over medium-high heat and stir until the sugar melts, turns golden brown, and bubbles: do not stir once the mixture starts to bubble. Remove from the heat and add the almonds one at a time and quickly turn with a fork until coated; if the caramel hardens, return the pan to the heat. Transfer each almond to a lightly buttered cookie sheet once it is coated. Let stand until cool and firm.

2 To serve, slice the figs in half and arrange 4 halves on each plate. Coarsely chop the almonds by hand, reserving a few whole ones for garnish. Place a mound of bleu cheese on each plate and sprinkle with chopped almonds. Drizzle the figs very lightly with the oil and garnish with the reserved, whole almonds.

asparagus with melted butter

ingredients

SERVES 2

16–20 stalks of asparagus,
   trimmed to about
   8 inches/20 cm
3 oz/85 g unsalted butter,
   melted
sea salt and pepper, to serve

method

1 Remove some of the base of the asparagus stalks with a potato peeler if they are rather thick. Tie the stalks together with string or use a wire basket so that they can easily be removed from the pan without damage.

2 Bring a large pan of salted water to a boil and plunge in the stalks. Cover with a lid and cook for 4–5 minutes. Pierce one stalk near the base with a sharp knife. If it is fairly soft remove from the heat at once. Do not overcook asparagus or the tender tips will fall off.

3 Drain the asparagus thoroughly and serve on large warmed plates with the butter poured over. Both the butter and the asparagus should be warm rather than hot. Serve with sea salt and pepper for sprinkling.

zucchini fritters with yogurt dip

ingredients

SERVES 4

2–3 zucchini, about 14 oz/400 g

1 garlic clove, crushed

3 scallions, finely sliced

4^1/$_2$ oz/125 g feta cheese,
    crumbled

2 tbsp finely chopped
    fresh parsley

2 tbsp finely chopped
    fresh mint

1 tbsp finely chopped fresh dill

^{1}/$_2$ tsp freshly grated nutmeg

2 tbsp all-purpose flour

pepper

2 eggs

2 tbsp olive oil

1 lemon, cut into fourths,
    to garnish

yogurt dip

9 oz/250 g/scant 1^1/$_4$ cups
    strained plain yogurt

^{1}/$_4$ cucumber, diced

1 tbsp finely chopped fresh dill

pepper

method

1 Grate the zucchini straight onto a clean dish towel and cover with another. Pat well and let stand for 10 minutes until the zucchini are dry.

2 Meanwhile, to make the dip, mix the yogurt, cucumber, dill, and pepper in a serving bowl. Cover and let chill.

3 Tip the zucchini into a large bowl. Stir in the garlic, scallions, cheese, herbs, nutmeg, flour, and pepper. Beat the eggs in a separate bowl and stir into the zucchini mixture—the batter will be quite lumpy and uneven but this is fine.

4 Heat the oil in a large, wide pan over medium heat. Drop 4 tablespoonfuls of the batter into the skillet, with space in between, and cook for 2–3 minutes on each side. Remove, drain on paper towels, and keep warm. Cook the second batch of fritters in the same way. (There should be 8 fritters in total.)

5 Serve the fritters hot with the dip, garnished with lemon fourths.

cheese & herb soufflés with sautéed mushrooms

ingredients

MAKES 6 SOUFFLÉS

2 oz/55 g butter, plus extra, melted, for greasing

1^{1}/$_{2}$ oz/40 g/^{1}/$_{3}$ cup all-purpose flour

5 fl oz/150 ml/^{2}/$_{3}$ cup milk

9 oz/250 g/generous 1 cup ricotta cheese

4 eggs, separated, plus 2 egg whites

2 tbsp finely chopped fresh parsley

2 tbsp finely chopped fresh thyme

1 tbsp finely chopped fresh rosemary

salt and pepper

7 fl oz/200 ml/scant 1 cup light cream

6 tbsp grated Parmesan cheese

sautéed white mushrooms, to serve

method

1 Brush 6 x 3^{1}/$_{2}$-inch/9-cm soufflé dishes well with melted butter and set aside. Melt the butter in a medium pan, add the flour, and cook for 30 seconds, stirring constantly. Whisk in the milk and continue whisking over low heat until the mixture thickens. Cook for an additional 30 seconds. Remove from the heat and beat in the ricotta. Add the egg yolks and herbs and season well with salt and pepper.

2 Beat the egg whites in a clean bowl until they form stiff peaks and gently fold them through the ricotta mixture. Spoon into the prepared dishes, filling them just to the top. Place in a baking dish and pour in enough boiling water to come halfway up the sides of the dishes. Bake the soufflés in a preheated oven, 350°F/180°C, for 15–20 minutes, or until well risen and browned. Remove from the oven, let cool for 10 minutes, then gently ease out of their molds. Place in a lightly greased ovenproof dish and cover with plastic wrap.

3 Increase the oven temperature to 400°F/ 200°C. Remove the plastic wrap and pour the cream evenly over the soufflés, sprinkle with Parmesan, and return to the oven for an additional 15 minutes. Serve at once with sautéed mushrooms.

artichokes with vièrge sauce

ingredients

SERVES 4

4 large globe artichokes

$1/2$ lemon, sliced

salt

vièrge sauce

3 large beefsteak tomatoes,
    peeled and seeded,
    then finely diced

4 scallions, very finely chopped

6 tbsp chopped fresh herbs,
    such as basil, chervil,
    chives, mint, flat-leaf
    parsley, or tarragon

5 fl oz/150 ml/$2/3$ cup
    full-flavored extra-virgin
    olive oil

pinch of sugar

salt and pepper

method

1 To prepare the artichokes, cut off the stems and trim the bottom so that they will stand upright on the plate. Use scissors to snip the leaf tips off each one, then drop in a large bowl of water with 2 of the lemon slices while the others are being prepared.

2 Select a pan large enough to hold the 4 artichokes upright and half-fill with salted water and the remaining lemon slices. Bring the water to a boil, then add the artichokes and place a heatproof plate on top to keep them submerged. Reduce the heat to a low boil and continue boiling the artichokes for 25–35 minutes, depending on their size, until the bottom leaves pull out easily.

3 While the artichokes are cooking, prepare the vièrge sauce. Put the tomatoes, scallions, herbs, oil, sugar, salt, and pepper in a pan and set aside for the flavors to blend.

4 When the artichokes are tender, drain them upside-down on paper towels, then transfer to individual plates. Heat the sauce very gently until it is just warm, then spoon it equally over the artichokes to serve.

sweet potato, mint & feta patties

ingredients

SERVES 4

1 lb 5 oz/600 g sweet potatoes, peeled and grated

1 egg, lightly beaten

$1/3$ cup all-purpose flour

$2^{1}/2$ oz/70 g butter, melted

$3^{1}/2$ oz/100 g feta cheese, crumbled

3 tbsp chopped fresh mint

salt and pepper

1 tbsp vegetable oil

4 tbsp sour cream

2 tbsp chopped fresh parsley, to garnish

method

1 Mix the grated sweet potato with the egg, flour, melted butter, feta, and mint until well combined. Season the mixture with salt and pepper.

2 Heat the oil in a large nonstick skillet over medium heat. Spoon large tablespoons of the mixture into patties, flattening slightly, and cook on both sides in batches until golden.

3 Slide the patties onto a cookie sheet covered with parchment paper and bake in a preheated oven, 325°F/160°C, for 15 minutes, or until crisp. Place 2 patties on each plate, top with a tablespoon of sour cream, and garnish with a little chopped parsley. Serve at once.

stuffed portobello mushrooms

ingredients

SERVES 4

12 large portobello mushrooms, wiped over and stems removed

2 tbsp corn oil, plus extra for oiling

1 fennel bulb, stalks removed, finely chopped

$3^{1}/_{2}$ oz/100 g/scant $^{1}/_{2}$ cup sun-dried tomatoes, finely chopped

2 garlic cloves, crushed

$4^{1}/_{2}$ oz/125 g/generous 1 cup grated fontina cheese

$1^{3}/_{4}$ oz/50 g/scant $^{1}/_{2}$ cup freshly grated Parmesan cheese

3 tbsp chopped fresh basil

salt and pepper

1 tbsp olive oil

fresh Parmesan cheese shavings

1 tbsp chopped fresh parsley, to serve

method

1 Place 8 of the mushrooms, cup-side up, in a large, lightly oiled ovenproof dish and chop the remaining 4 mushrooms finely.

2 Heat the corn oil in a nonstick skillet, add the chopped mushrooms, fennel, sun-dried tomatoes, and garlic and cook over low heat until the vegetables are soft, but not browned. Remove from the heat and let cool.

3 When cool, add the cheeses, basil, salt, and pepper. Mix well. Brush the mushrooms lightly with the olive oil and fill each cavity with a spoonful of the vegetable filling. Bake in a preheated oven, 350°F/180°C, for 20–25 minutes, or until the mushrooms are tender and the filling is heated through.

4 Top with Parmesan shavings and parsley and serve at once, allowing 2 mushrooms for each person.

falafel with tahini sauce

ingredients

SERVES 4

1 lb/450 g canned cannellini
    beans, drained
12 oz/350 g canned
    chickpeas, drained
1 onion, finely chopped
2 garlic cloves, chopped
1 small fresh red chile,
    seeded and chopped
1 tsp baking powder
1 oz/25 g fresh parsley,
    chopped, plus extra
    sprigs to garnish
pinch of cayenne
2 tbsp water
salt and pepper
vegetable oil, for deep-frying
pita bread, thick plain yogurt
    or yogurt dip (see page
    38), and lemon wedges,
    to serve

tahini sauce

7 fl oz/200 ml/scant 1 cup
    sesame seed paste
1 garlic clove, chopped
1–2 tbsp water
2–3 tsp lemon juice, to taste

method

1 To make the tahini sauce, put the sesame seed paste and garlic in a bowl. Gradually stir in the water until a fairly smooth consistency is reached, then stir in the lemon juice. Add more water or lemon juice, if necessary. Cover with plastic wrap and let chill in the refrigerator until required.

2 To make the falafel, rinse and drain the beans and chickpeas. Put them in a food processor with the onion, garlic, chile, baking powder, chopped parsley, and cayenne pepper. Process to a coarse paste, then add the water and season with plenty of salt and pepper. Process again briefly.

3 Heat about 2$1/2$ inches/6 cm of oil in a deep-fat fryer, large, heavy-bottom pan, or wok over high heat. Deep-fry rounded tablespoonfuls of the mixture in batches for 2–2$1/2$ minutes until golden and crispy on the outside. Remove with a slotted spoon and drain well on paper towels. Serve hot or cold, garnished with parsley sprigs and accompanied by the tahini sauce, pita bread, yogurt or yogurt dip, and lemon wedges.

black bean nachos

ingredients

SERVES 4

8 oz/225 g/1 cup dried black
    beans, or canned black
    beans, drained
6–8 oz/175–225 g/
    $1^{1}/_2$–2 cups grated
    cheese, such as Cheddar,
    fontina, romano, Asiago,
    or a combination
about $^1/_4$ tsp cumin seeds or
    ground cumin
about 4 tbsp sour cream
thinly sliced pickled jalapeño
    chiles (optional)
1 tbsp chopped fresh cilantro
handful of shredded lettuce
tortilla chips, to serve

method

1 If using dried black beans, soak the beans overnight, then drain. Put into a pan, cover with water, and bring to a boil. Boil for 10 minutes, then reduce the heat and simmer for $1^{1}/_2$ hours, or until tender. Drain well.

2 Spread the beans in a shallow ovenproof dish, then scatter the cheese over the top. Sprinkle with cumin to taste.

3 Bake in a preheated oven, 375°F/190°C, for 10–15 minutes, or until the beans are cooked through and the cheese is bubbly and melted.

4 Remove from the oven and spoon the sour cream on top. Add the chiles, if using, and sprinkle with cilantro and lettuce.

5 Arrange the tortilla chips around the beans, placing them in the mixture. Serve the nachos at once.

beans, nuts & bean curd

Beans, nuts, and bean curd are three of the most important ingredients in a vegetarian diet. Beans are full of protein, and come in a variety of shapes and colors, from the dark red kidney bean, named after its distinctive shape, to the large white haricot bean. They make a filling, satisfying base for stews and curries. Chickpeas are eaten whole and also ground into flour—try Mixed Vegetable Curry with Chickpea Pancakes. Lentils are a useful substitute for ground meat, so if you love Italian food, try Lentil Bolognese for a new twist on a classic dish.

For maximum nutritional benefit, eat beans and lentils with a grain food such as rice or whole wheat bread—Kidney Bean Risotto is an ideal combination.

Nuts are also packed with goodness, and are beneficial to the nervous system. Serve Nutty Bleu Cheese Roast or Vegetable & Hazelnut Loaf with roast potatoes and plenty of vegetables to replace a traditional meat roast.

Bean curd has a bland taste that is transformed when it is cooked with strong flavorings, such as garlic and chile. It comes in blocks that can be cut into smaller chunks and is a lowfat food that is perfect for vegetarians. Buckwheat Noodle Salad with Smoked Bean Curd is gluten-free, dairy-free, and delicious!

mexican three-bean chili stew

ingredients

SERVES 6

5 oz/140 g/generous ³/₄ cup
    each dried black beans,
    cannellini beans and
    pinto beans, soaked
    overnight in separate
    bowls in water to cover

2 tbsp olive oil

1 large onion, finely chopped

2 red bell peppers, seeded
    and diced

2 garlic cloves, very finely
    chopped

¹/₂ tsp cumin seeds, crushed

1 tsp coriander seeds,
    crushed

1 tsp dried oregano

¹/₂–2 tsp chili powder

3 tbsp tomato paste

1 lb 12 oz/800 g canned
    chopped tomatoes

1 tsp sugar

1 tsp salt

20 fl oz/625 ml/2¹/₂ cups
    vegetable stock

3 tbsp chopped fresh cilantro

method

1 Drain the beans, put in separate pans, and cover with cold water. Bring to a boil and boil vigorously for 10–15 minutes, then reduce the heat and let simmer for 35–45 minutes until just tender. Drain and set aside.

2 Heat the oil in a large, heavy-bottom pan over medium heat. Add the onion and bell peppers and cook, stirring frequently, for 5 minutes, or until softened.

3 Add the garlic, cumin and coriander seeds, and oregano and cook, stirring, for 30 seconds until the garlic is beginning to color. Add the chili powder and tomato paste and cook, stirring, for 1 minute. Add the tomatoes, sugar, salt, beans, and stock. Bring to a boil, then reduce the heat, cover, and let simmer, stirring occasionally, for 45 minutes.

4 Stir in the fresh cilantro. Ladle into individual warmed bowls and serve immediately.

sweet-&-sour vegetables with cashews

ingredients

SERVES 4

1 tbsp vegetable or peanut oil

1 tsp chili oil

2 onions, sliced

2 carrots, thinly sliced

2 zucchini, thinly sliced

4 oz/115 g broccoli,
    cut into florets

4 oz/115 g white mushrooms,
    sliced

4 oz/115 g small bok choy,
    halved

2 tbsp jaggery or brown sugar

2 tbsp Thai soy sauce

1 tbsp rice vinegar

2 oz/55 g/generous $^1/_3$ cup
    cashews

method

1 Heat both the oils in a preheated wok or skillet, add the onions, and stir-fry for 1–2 minutes until beginning to soften.

2 Add the carrots, zucchini, and broccoli and stir-fry for 2–3 minutes. Add the mushrooms, bok choy, sugar, soy sauce, and vinegar and stir-fry for 1–2 minutes.

3 Meanwhile, heat a dry, heavy-bottom skillet over high heat, add the cashews, and cook, shaking the skillet frequently, until lightly toasted. Sprinkle the cashews over the stir-fry and serve immediately.

spicy fragrant black bean chili

ingredients

SERVES 4

14 oz/400 g/2^1/$_4$ cups dried
   black beans
2 tbsp olive oil
1 onion, chopped
5 garlic cloves, coarsely
   chopped
^{1}/$_2$–1 tsp ground cumin
^{1}/$_2$–1 tsp mild red chili powder
1 red bell pepper, diced
1 carrot, diced
14 oz/400 g fresh tomatoes,
   diced, or canned, chopped
1 bunch fresh cilantro,
   coarsely chopped
salt and pepper

method

1 Soak the beans overnight, then drain. Place in a pan, cover with water, and bring to a boil. Boil for 10 minutes, then reduce the heat and simmer for 1^1/2 hours, or until tender. Drain well, reserving 1 cup of the cooking liquid.

2 Heat the oil in a skillet. Add the onion and garlic and cook for 2 minutes, stirring. Cook, stirring occasionally, until the onion is softened.

3 Stir in the cumin and chili powder and continue to cook for a moment or two. Add the red bell pepper, carrot, and tomatoes. Cook over medium heat for 5 minutes.

4 Add half the cilantro and the beans and their reserved liquid. Season with salt and pepper. Simmer for 30–45 minutes, or until very flavorful and thickened.

5 Stir in the remaining cilantro, adjust the seasoning, and serve at once.

provençal bean stew

ingredients

SERVES 4

12 oz/350 g/2 cups dried
   pinto beans, soaked
   overnight in water
   to cover
2 tbsp olive oil
2 onions, sliced
2 garlic cloves, finely chopped
1 red bell pepper, seeded and
   sliced
1 yellow bell pepper, seeded
   and sliced
14 oz/400 g canned chopped
   tomatoes
2 tbsp tomato paste
1 tbsp torn fresh basil leaves
2 tsp chopped fresh thyme
2 tsp chopped fresh rosemary
1 bay leaf
salt and pepper
2 oz/55 g/^{1}/$_3$ cup black olives,
   pitted and halved
2 tbsp chopped fresh parsley,
   to garnish

method

1 Drain the beans. Place in a large pan, add enough cold water to cover, and bring to a boil. Reduce the heat, then cover and let simmer for 1^1/4–1^1/2 hours until almost tender. Drain, reserving 10 fl oz/300 ml/1^1/4 cups of the cooking liquid.

2 Heat the oil in a heavy-bottom pan over medium heat. Add the onions and cook, stirring frequently, for 5 minutes, or until softened. Add the garlic and bell peppers and cook, stirring occasionally, for 10 minutes.

3 Add the tomatoes and their can juices, the reserved cooking liquid, tomato paste, basil, thyme, rosemary, bay leaf, and beans. Season with salt and pepper. Cover and simmer for 40 minutes. Add the olives and simmer for 5 minutes. Transfer to a warmed serving dish, sprinkle with the parsley, and serve immediately.

boston beans

ingredients

SERVES 8

1 lb 2 oz/500 g dried
   cannellini beans, soaked
   overnight in water to cover
2 onions, chopped
2 large tomatoes, peeled and
   chopped
2 tsp American mustard
2 tbsp molasses
salt and pepper

method

1 Drain the beans and put in a large pan. Add enough cold water to cover and bring to a boil. Reduce the heat and simmer for 15 minutes. Drain, reserving 10 fl oz/300 ml/1 1/4 cups of the cooking liquid. Transfer the beans to a large casserole and add the onions.

2 Return the reserved cooking liquid to the pan and add the tomatoes. Bring to a boil, then reduce the heat and let simmer for 10 minutes. Remove from the heat, stir in the mustard and molasses, and season with salt and pepper.

3 Pour the mixture into the casserole, stir, and bake in a preheated oven, 275°F/140°C, for 5 hours. Serve hot.

baked portobello mushrooms

ingredients

SERVES 4

4 large portobello mushrooms

7 oz/200 g canned red kidney
    beans, drained and rinsed

4 scallions, chopped

1 fresh red jalapeño chile,
    seeded and finely chopped

1 tbsp finely grated lemon rind

1 tbsp chopped fresh flatleaf
    parsley, plus extra sprigs
    to garnish

salt and pepper

3 oz/85 g zucchini, coarsely
    grated

3 oz/85 g carrots, coarsely
    grated

2 oz/55 g/$^{3}/_{8}$ cup pine nuts,
    toasted

1$^{1}/_{2}$ oz/40 g/generous $^{1}/_{4}$ cup
    raisins

10 fl oz/300 ml/1$^{1}/_{4}$ cups
    vegetable stock

sauce

5 fl oz/150 ml/$^{2}/_{3}$ cup strained
    plain yogurt

1 tbsp chopped fresh parsley,
    plus extra to garnish

1 tbsp grated lemon rind

salt and pepper

method

1 Peel the mushrooms and carefully remove the stalks. Trim and rinse the stalks.

2 Put the mushroom stalks, beans, scallions, chile, lemon rind, parsley, salt, and pepper into a food processor and process for 2 minutes.

3 Scrape the mixture into a bowl and add the zucchini, carrots, pine nuts, and raisins. Mix well and use to stuff the mushroom cups.

4 Arrange the stuffed mushrooms in an ovenproof dish, pour the stock around them, and cover with foil. Bake in a preheated oven, 350°F/180°C, for 30 minutes, removing the foil for the last 10 minutes of the cooking time.

5 Meanwhile, to make the sauce, blend all the ingredients together in a small serving dish.

6 Serve the mushrooms hot with the sauce, garnished with parsley sprigs.

red & white bean curry

ingredients

SERVES 4

3 oz/85 g/$^{1}/_{2}$ cup red
   kidney beans

3 oz/85 g/$^{1}/_{2}$ cup haricot
   beans

2 oz/55 g/$^{1}/_{3}$ cup black-eye
   peas

2 tbsp ghee or vegetable oil

1 tsp black mustard seeds

1 tsp cumin seeds

1 onion, finely chopped

1 tsp garlic paste

1 tsp ginger paste

2 tbsp curry paste

2 fresh green chiles, seeded
   and chopped

14 oz/400 g canned tomatoes

2 tbsp tomato paste

4–5 fl oz/125–150 ml/
   $^{1}/_{2}$–$^{2}/_{3}$ cup water (optional)

salt

2 tbsp chopped fresh cilantro,
   plus extra to garnish

method

1 Place all the beans in a large bowl, add enough cold water to cover, and let soak for at least 4 hours or overnight.

2 Drain the beans and place in a large, heavy-bottom pan. Add enough cold water to cover and bring to a boil over high heat. Boil vigorously for 15 minutes, then reduce the heat, cover, and let simmer for 1$^{1}/_{2}$ hours, or until the beans are tender.

3 Heat the ghee in a separate large pan. Add the mustard seeds and cumin seeds and cook over low heat, stirring, for 2 minutes, or until they give off their aroma. Add the onion and cook, stirring frequently, for 5 minutes, or until softened. Add the garlic paste, ginger paste, curry paste, and chiles and cook, stirring, for 2 minutes. Stir in the tomatoes and their can juices and the tomato paste. If the sauce seems thick, add the water. Break up the tomatoes with a wooden spoon. Season with salt and let simmer for 5 minutes.

4 Drain the beans and add them to the sauce, then stir in the chopped cilantro. Cover and let simmer for an additional 30 minutes, or until the beans are tender and the sauce has thickened. Garnish with extra chopped cilantro and serve immediately.

kidney bean risotto

ingredients

SERVES 4

4 tbsp olive oil

1 onion, chopped

2 garlic cloves, finely chopped

6 oz/175 g/generous $^3/_4$ cup
   brown rice

20 fl oz/625 ml/2$^1/_2$ cups
   vegetable stock

salt and pepper

1 red bell pepper, seeded
   and chopped

2 celery stalks, sliced

8 oz/225 g cremini
   mushrooms, thinly sliced

15 oz/425 g canned red
   kidney beans, drained
   and rinsed

3 tbsp chopped fresh parsley,
   plus extra to garnish

2 oz/55 g/scant $^3/_8$ cup
   cashews

method

1 Heat half the oil in a large, heavy-bottom pan. Add the onion and cook, stirring occasionally, for 5 minutes, or until softened. Add half the garlic and cook, stirring frequently, for 2 minutes, then add the rice and stir for 1 minute, or until the grains are thoroughly coated with the oil.

2 Add the stock and a pinch of salt and bring to a boil, stirring constantly. Reduce the heat, cover, and let simmer for 35–40 minutes, or until all the liquid has been absorbed.

3 Meanwhile, heat the remaining oil in a heavy-bottom skillet. Add the bell pepper and celery and cook, stirring frequently, for 5 minutes. Add the sliced mushrooms and the remaining garlic and cook, stirring frequently, for 4–5 minutes.

4 Stir the rice into the skillet. Add the beans, parsley, and cashews. Season with salt and pepper and cook, stirring constantly, until hot. Transfer to a warmed serving dish, sprinkle with extra parsley, and serve at once.

mixed vegetable curry with chickpea pancakes

ingredients

SERVES 4

7 oz/200 g carrots
10¹/₂ oz/300 g potatoes
2 tbsp vegetable oil
1¹/₂ tsp cumin seeds
seeds from 5 green
    cardamom pods
1¹/₂ tsp mustard seeds
2 onions, grated
1 tsp ground turmeric
1 tsp ground coriander
1¹/₂ tsp chili powder
1 bay leaf
1 tbsp grated fresh gingerroot
2 large garlic cloves, crushed
9 fl oz/250 ml/scant 1¹/₄ cups
    strained tomatoes
7 fl oz/200 ml/scant 1 cup
    vegetable stock
4 oz/115 g/1 cup frozen peas
4 oz/115 g frozen spinach
    leaves

chickpea pancakes

8 oz/225 g/generous
    1¹/₂ cups chickpea flour
1 tsp salt
¹/₂ tsp baking soda
4 fl oz/400 ml/1³/₄ cups water
vegetable oil, for cooking

method

1 To make the pancakes, sift the flour, salt, and baking soda into a large mixing bowl. Make a well in the center and add the water. Using a balloon whisk, gradually mix the flour into the water to form a smooth batter. Let stand for 15 minutes.

2 Heat enough oil to cover the bottom of a skillet over medium heat. Add a small quantity of batter to the skillet, and cook for 3 minutes on one side, then turn over and cook the other side until golden. Keep warm while you repeat with the remaining batter to make 8 pancakes.

3 Meanwhile, cut the carrots into chunks and the potatoes into fourths. Place in a steamer and steam until just tender.

4 Heat the oil in a large pan over medium heat and fry the cumin, cardamom, and mustard seeds until they start to sizzle. Add the onions, partially cover, and cook over medium-low heat, stirring frequently, until soft and golden.

5 Add the other spices, bay leaf, gingerroot, and garlic and cook, stirring, for 1 minute. Add the strained tomatoes, stock, carrots, and potatoes, partially cover, and cook for 10–15 minutes, or until the vegetables are tender. Add the peas and spinach, then cook for 2–3 minutes. Serve with the warm pancakes.

spinach with chickpeas

ingredients

SERVES 4–6

2 tbsp olive oil

1 large garlic clove, cut in half

1 medium onion,
    chopped finely

$1/2$ tsp cumin

pinch cayenne pepper

pinch turmeric

1 lb 12 oz/800 g canned
    chickpeas, drained
    and rinsed

18 oz/500 g baby spinach
    leaves, rinsed and shaken
    dry

2 pimientos del piquillo,
    drained and sliced

salt and pepper

method

1 Heat the oil in a large, lidded skillet over medium-high heat. Add the garlic and cook for 2 minutes, or until golden, but not brown. Remove with a slotted spoon and discard.

2 Add the onion and cumin, cayenne and turmeric and cook, stirring, for about 5 minutes until soft. Add the chickpeas and stir around until they are lightly colored with the turmeric and cayenne.

3 Stir in the spinach with just the water clinging to its leaves. Cover and cook for 4–5 minutes until wilted. Uncover, stir in the pimientos del piquillo and continue cooking, stirring gently, until all the liquid evaporates. Season with salt and pepper and serve.

chickpea curry

ingredients

SERVES 4

6 tbsp vegetable oil

2 onions, sliced

1 tsp finely chopped fresh
    gingerroot

1 tsp ground cumin

1 tsp ground coriander

1 tsp fresh garlic, crushed

1 tsp chili powder

2 fresh green chiles

2–3 tbsp fresh cilantro leaves

5 fl oz/150 ml/^{2}/$_3$ cup water

1 large potato

14 oz/400 g canned
    chickpeas, drained

1 tbsp lemon juice

method

1 Heat the vegetable oil in a large, heavy-bottom pan. Add the onions and cook, stirring occasionally, until golden. Reduce the heat, add the gingerroot, ground cumin, ground coriander, garlic, chili powder, fresh green chiles, and fresh cilantro leaves and stir-fry for 2 minutes.

2 Add the water to the mixture in the pan and stir to mix.

3 Using a sharp knife, cut the potato into dice, then add, with the chickpeas, to the pan. Cover and let simmer, stirring occasionally, for 5–7 minutes.

4 Sprinkle the lemon juice over the curry. Transfer the chickpea curry to serving dishes and serve hot.

chile bean cakes with avocado salsa

ingredients

SERVES 4

2 oz/55 g/$^3/_8$ cup pine nuts

15 oz/425 g canned mixed
   beans, drained and rinsed

$^1/_2$ red onion, finely chopped

1 tbsp tomato paste

$^1/_2$ fresh red chile, seeded
   and finely chopped

2 oz/55 g/1 cup fresh brown
   bread crumbs

1 egg, beaten

1 tbsp finely chopped fresh
   cilantro

2 tbsp corn oil

1 lime, cut into fourths,
   to garnish

4 toasted whole-wheat bread
   rolls, to serve (optional)

salsa

1 avocado, pitted, peeled,
   and chopped

3$^1/_2$ oz/100 g tomatoes,
   seeded and chopped

2 garlic cloves, crushed

2 tbsp finely chopped fresh
   cilantro

1 tbsp olive oil

pepper

juice of $^1/_2$ lime

method

1 Heat a nonstick skillet over medium heat, add the pine nuts, and cook, turning, until just browned. Tip into a bowl and set aside.

2 Put the beans into a large bowl and coarsely mash. Add the onion, tomato paste, chile, pine nuts, and half the bread crumbs and mix well. Add half the egg and the cilantro and mash together, adding a little more egg, if needed, to bind the mixture. Form the mixture into 4 flat cakes. Coat with the remaining bread crumbs, cover, and let chill in the refrigerator for 30 minutes.

3 To make the salsa, mix all the ingredients together in a serving bowl, cover, and let chill in the refrigerator until required.

4 Heat the oil in a skillet over medium heat, add the bean cakes, and cook for 4–5 minutes on each side, or until crisp and heated through. Remove from the skillet and drain on paper towels.

5 Serve each bean cake in a toasted whole-wheat roll, if desired, with the salsa, garnished with a lime fourth.

bean burgers

ingredients

SERVES 4

1 tbsp sunflower oil, plus
    extra for brushing
1 onion, finely chopped
1 garlic clove, finely chopped
1 tsp ground coriander
1 tsp ground cumin
4 oz/115 g white mushrooms,
    finely chopped
15 oz/425 g canned pinto or
    red kidney beans,
    drained and rinsed
2 tbsp chopped fresh flat-leaf
    parsley
salt and pepper
all-purpose flour, for dusting
hamburger buns
salad, to serve

method

1 Heat the oil in a heavy-bottom skillet over medium heat. Add the onion and cook, stirring frequently, for 5 minutes, or until softened. Add the garlic, coriander, and cumin and cook, stirring, for an additional minute. Add the mushrooms and cook, stirring frequently, for 4–5 minutes until all the liquid has evaporated. Transfer to a bowl.

2 Put the beans in a small bowl and mash with a fork. Stir into the mushroom mixture with the parsley and season with salt and pepper.

3 Preheat the broiler to medium-high. Divide the mixture equally into 4 portions, dust lightly with flour, and shape into flat, round patties. Brush with oil and cook under the broiler for 4–5 minutes on each side. Serve in hamburger buns with salad.

toasted pine nut & vegetable couscous

ingredients

SERVES 4

4 oz/115 g/generous ¹/₂ cup
   dried green lentils
2 oz/55 g/³/₈ cup pine nuts
1 tbsp olive oil
1 onion, diced
2 garlic cloves, crushed
10 oz/280 g zucchini, sliced
9 oz/250 g tomatoes, chopped
14 oz/400 g canned artichoke
   hearts, drained and cut in
   half lengthwise
9 oz/250 g/generous
   1¹/₄ cups couscous
16 fl oz/500 ml/2 cups
   vegetable stock
3 tbsp torn fresh basil leaves,
   plus extra leaves to garnish
pepper

method

1 Put the lentils into a pan with plenty of cold water, bring to a boil, and boil rapidly for 10 minutes. Reduce the heat, cover, and let simmer for 15 minutes, or until tender.

2 Meanwhile, preheat the broiler to medium. Spread the pine nuts out in a single layer on a cookie sheet and toast under the preheated broiler, turning to brown evenly—watch constantly because they brown very quickly. Tip the pine nuts into a small dish and set aside.

3 Heat the oil in a skillet over medium heat, add the onion, garlic, and zucchini and cook, stirring frequently, for 8–10 minutes, or until tender and the zucchini have browned slightly. Add the tomatoes and artichoke halves and heat through thoroughly for 5 minutes.

4 Meanwhile, put the couscous into a heatproof bowl. Bring the stock to a boil in a pan and pour over the couscous, cover, and let stand for 10 minutes until the couscous absorbs the stock and becomes tender.

5 Drain the lentils and stir into the couscous. Stir in the torn basil leaves and season well with pepper. Transfer to a warmed serving dish and spoon over the cooked vegetables. Sprinkle the pine nuts over the top, garnish with basil leaves, and serve at once.

warm red lentil salad with goat cheese

ingredients

SERVES 4

2 tbsp olive oil

2 tsp cumin seeds

2 garlic cloves, crushed

2 tsp grated fresh gingerroot

10^{1}/$_{2}$ oz/300 g/1^{1}/$_{2}$ cups
   split red lentils

24 fl oz/750 ml/3 cups
   vegetable stock

2 tbsp chopped fresh mint

2 tbsp chopped fresh cilantro

2 red onions, thinly sliced

7 oz/200 g baby spinach
   leaves

1 tsp hazelnut oil

5^{1}/$_{2}$ oz/150 g soft goat cheese

4 tbsp strained plain yogurt

pepper

1 lemon, cut into fourths,
   to garnish

toasted rye bread, to serve

method

1 Heat half the olive oil in a large pan over medium heat, add the cumin seeds, garlic, and gingerroot and cook for 2 minutes, stirring constantly.

2 Stir in the lentils, then add the stock, a ladleful at a time, until it is all absorbed, stirring constantly—this will take about 20 minutes. Remove from the heat and stir in the herbs.

3 Meanwhile, heat the remaining olive oil in a skillet over medium heat, add the onions, and cook, stirring frequently, for 10 minutes, or until soft and lightly browned.

4 Toss the spinach in the hazelnut oil in a bowl, then divide among 4 serving plates.

5 Mash the goat cheese with the yogurt in a small bowl and season with pepper.

6 Divide the lentils among the serving plates and top with the onions and goat cheese mixture. Garnish with lemon fourths and serve with toasted rye bread.

lentil bolognese

ingredients

SERVES 4

1 tsp vegetable oil

1 tsp minced garlic

1 oz/25 g onion, finely
chopped

1 oz/25 g leek, finely chopped

1 oz/25 g celery, finely chopped

1 oz/25 g green bell pepper,
seeded and finely
chopped

1 oz/25 g carrot, finely
chopped

1 oz/25 g zucchini, finely
chopped

3 oz/85 g flat mushrooms,
diced

4 tbsp red wine

pinch of dried thyme

14 oz/400 g canned tomatoes,
chopped, strained through
a colander, and the juice
and pulp reserved
separately

4 tbsp dried Puy or green
lentils, cooked

pepper, to taste

2 tsp lemon juice

1 tsp sugar

3 tbsp chopped fresh basil,
plus extra sprigs to garnish

freshly cooked spaghetti,
to serve

method

1 Heat a pan over a low heat, add the oil and garlic and cook, stirring, until golden brown. Add all the vegetables, except the mushrooms, increase the heat to medium and cook, stirring occasionally, for 10–12 minutes, or until softened and there is no liquid from the vegetables left in the pan. Add the mushrooms.

2 Increase the heat to high, add the wine, and cook for 2 minutes. Add the thyme and the juice from the tomatoes and cook until reduced by half.

3 Add the lentils and pepper, stir in the tomatoes, and cook for a further 3–4 minutes. Remove the pan from the heat and stir in the lemon juice, sugar, and basil.

4 Serve the sauce with freshly cooked spaghetti, garnished with basil sprigs.

lentil, shallot & mushroom pie

ingredients

SERVES 6

6 oz/175 g/scant 1 cup
   Puy or green lentils
2 bay leaves
6 shallots, sliced
40 fl oz/1.25 liters/5 cups
   vegetable stock
salt and pepper
4 tbsp butter
8 oz/225 g/scant $1^1/_4$ cups
   long-grain rice
8 sheets filo pastry,
   thawed if frozen
2 tbsp chopped fresh parsley
2 tsp chopped fresh fennel
   or savory
4 eggs, 1 beaten and
   3 hard-cooked and sliced
8 oz/225 g portobello
   mushrooms, sliced

method

1 Put the lentils, bay leaves, and half the shallots in a large, heavy-bottom pan. Add half the stock and bring to a boil. Reduce the heat and let simmer for 25 minutes, or until the lentils are tender. Remove from the heat, season with salt and pepper, and let cool completely.

2 Melt half the butter in a heavy-bottom pan over medium heat, add the remaining shallots, and cook, stirring frequently, until softened. Add the rice and cook, stirring, for 1 minute, then add the remaining stock. Season and bring to a boil. Reduce the heat, cover, and let simmer for 15 minutes. Remove from the heat and let cool completely.

3 Melt the remaining butter over low heat, then brush an ovenproof dish with a little of it. Arrange the filo sheets in the dish with the sides overhanging, brushing each sheet with melted butter. Add the parsley, fennel, and beaten egg to the rice mixture. Make layers of rice, hard-cooked egg, lentils, and mushrooms in the dish, seasoning each layer. Scrunch up the filo sheets into folds on top of the pie. Brush with melted butter and let chill for 15 minutes. Bake in a preheated oven, 375°F/ 190°C, for 45 minutes. Let stand for 10 minutes before serving.

baby corn with dal

ingredients

SERVES 4

8 oz/225 g/generous 1 cup
   red split lentils
2 tbsp vegetable oil
1 tsp cumin seeds
1 tsp ground coriander
$^1/_2$ tsp asafetida
1 fresh red chile, seeded and
   finely chopped
4 oz/115 g green beans,
   chopped, blanched,
   and drained
1 green bell pepper, seeded
   and chopped
4 oz/115 g baby corn, sliced
   diagonally
5 fl oz/150 ml/$^2/_3$ cup
   vegetable stock
2 tomatoes, seeded and
   chopped
1 tbsp chopped fresh cilantro
1 tbsp poppy seeds

method

1 Rinse the lentils 2–3 times in cold water. Put into a large pan and cover with cold water. Bring to a boil, then reduce the heat and let simmer for 15–20 minutes, or until tender. Drain, return to the pan, and keep warm.

2 Meanwhile, heat the oil in a separate pan over low heat, add the spices and chile, and cook for 2 minutes, stirring constantly. Add the beans, green bell pepper, and baby corn and cook for 2 minutes, stirring constantly.

3 Stir in the stock and bring to a boil, then reduce the heat and let simmer for 5 minutes, or until the vegetables are just tender.

4 Stir the vegetables and their liquid into the cooked lentils with the tomatoes and heat through for 5–8 minutes, or until piping hot.

5 Serve at once sprinkled with the cilantro and poppy seeds.

celery root, chestnut, spinach & feta filo pies

ingredients

SERVES 4

4 tbsp olive oil

2 garlic cloves, crushed

$1/2$ large or 1 whole small
head celery root, cut into
short thin sticks

9 oz/250 g baby spinach
leaves

3 oz/85 g/scant $1/2$ cup
cooked, peeled chestnuts,
coarsely chopped

7 oz/200 g feta cheese
(drained weight), crumbled

1 egg

2 tbsp pesto sauce

1 tbsp finely chopped fresh
parsley

pepper

4 sheets filo pastry,
about 13 x 7 inches/
32 x 18 cm each

method

1 Heat 1 tablespoon of the oil in a large skillet over medium heat, add the garlic, and cook for 1 minute, stirring constantly. Add the celery root and cook for 5 minutes, or until soft and browned. Remove from the skillet and keep warm.

2 Add 1 tablespoon of the remaining oil to the skillet, then add the spinach, cover, and cook for 2–3 minutes, or until the spinach has wilted. Uncover and cook until any liquid has evaporated.

3 Mix the garlic and celery root, spinach, chestnuts, cheese, egg, pesto, parsley, and pepper in a large bowl. Divide the mixture among 4 individual gratin dishes or put it all into 1 medium gratin dish.

4 Brush each sheet of filo with the remaining oil and arrange, slightly scrunched, on top of the celery root mixture. Bake in a preheated oven, 375°F/190°C, for 15–20 minutes, or until browned. Serve at once.

nutty bleu cheese roast

ingredients

SERVES 6–8

2 tbsp virgin olive oil,
plus extra for oiling

2 onions, one finely chopped
and one cut into
thin wedges

3–5 garlic cloves, crushed

2 celery stalks, finely sliced

6 oz/175 g/scant 1 cup
cooked and peeled
chestnuts

6 oz/175 g/generous 1 cup
mixed chopped nuts

2 oz/55 g/generous 1/2 cup
ground almonds

2 oz/55 g/1 cup fresh whole
wheat bread crumbs

8 oz/225 g bleu cheese,
crumbled

1 tbsp chopped fresh basil,
plus extra sprigs to garnish

1 egg, beaten

salt and pepper

1 red bell pepper, peeled,
seeded, and cut into
thin wedges

1 zucchini, about 4 oz/115 g,
cut into wedges

cherry tomatoes, to garnish

tomato ketchup, to serve

method

1 Heat 1 tablespoon of the oil in a skillet over medium heat, add the chopped onion, 1–2 of the garlic cloves, and the celery and cook for 5 minutes, stirring occasionally.

2 Remove from the skillet, drain through a strainer and transfer to a food processor with the nuts, bread crumbs, half the cheese, and the basil. Using the pulse button, blend the ingredients together, then slowly blend in the egg to form a stiff mixture. Season.

3 Heat the remaining oil in a skillet over medium heat, add the onion wedges, remaining garlic, red bell pepper, and zucchini and cook for 5 minutes, stirring frequently. Remove from the skillet, add salt and pepper, and drain through a strainer.

4 Place half the nut mixture in a lightly oiled 2-lb/900-g loaf pan and smooth the surface. Cover with the onion and bell pepper mixture and crumble over the remaining cheese. Top with the remaining nut mixture and press down firmly. Cover with foil. Bake in a preheated oven, 350°F/180°C, for 45 minutes. Remove the foil and bake for an additional 25–35 minutes, or until cooked and firm to the touch.

5 Remove from the oven, let cool in the pan for 5 minutes, then turn out and serve in slices garnished with basil sprigs, cherry tomatoes, and a little tomato ketchup.

vegetable & hazelnut loaf

ingredients

SERVES 4

2 tbsp sunflower oil, plus
    extra for oiling
1 onion, chopped
1 garlic clove, finely chopped
2 celery stalks, chopped
1 tbsp all-purpose flour
7 fl oz/200 ml/scant 1 cup
    strained canned tomatoes
4 oz/115 g/2 cups fresh
    whole wheat bread
    crumbs
2 carrots, grated
4 oz/115 g/^{3}/4 cup toasted
    hazelnuts, ground
1 tbsp dark soy sauce
2 tbsp chopped fresh cilantro
1 egg, lightly beaten
salt and pepper
mixed red and green lettuce
    leaves, to serve

method

1 Oil and line a 1-lb/450-g loaf pan. Heat the oil in a heavy-bottom skillet over medium heat. Add the onion and cook, stirring frequently, for 5 minutes, or until softened. Add the garlic and celery and cook, stirring frequently, for 5 minutes. Add the flour and cook, stirring constantly, for 1 minute. Gradually stir in the strained canned tomatoes and cook, stirring constantly, until thickened. Remove the skillet from the heat.

2 Put the bread crumbs, carrots, ground hazelnuts, soy sauce, and cilantro in a bowl. Add the tomato mixture and stir well. Let cool slightly, then beat in the egg and season with salt and pepper.

3 Spoon the mixture into the prepared pan and smooth the surface. Cover with foil and bake in a preheated oven, 350°F/180°C, for 1 hour. If serving hot, turn the loaf out on to a warmed serving dish and serve immediately with mixed red and green salad leaves. Alternatively, let the loaf cool in the pan before turning out.

buckwheat noodle salad with smoked bean curd

ingredients

SERVES 2

7 oz/200 g buckwheat noodles

9 oz/250 g firm smoked bean curd, drained weight

7 oz/200 g white cabbage, finely shredded

9 oz/250 g carrots, finely shredded

3 scallions, diagonally sliced

1 fresh red chile, seeded and finely sliced into circles

2 tbsp sesame seeds, lightly toasted

dressing

1 tsp grated fresh gingerroot

1 garlic clove, crushed

6 oz/175 g silken bean curd, drained weight

4 tsp tamari (wheat-free soy sauce)

2 tbsp sesame oil

4 tbsp hot water

salt

method

1 Cook the noodles in a large pan of lightly salted boiling water according to the package instructions. Drain and refresh under cold running water.

2 To make the dressing, blend the gingerroot, garlic, silken bean curd, tamari, oil, and water together in a small bowl until smooth and creamy. Season with salt.

3 Place the smoked bean curd in a steamer. Steam for 5 minutes, then cut into thin slices.

4 Meanwhile, put the cabbage, carrots, scallions, and chile into a bowl and toss to mix. To serve, arrange the noodles on serving plates and top with the carrot salad and slices of bean curd. Spoon over the dressing and sprinkle with sesame seeds.

thai bean curd cakes with chili dip

ingredients

SERVES 8

10^1/2 oz/300 g firm bean
    curd, drained weight,
    coarsely grated
1 lemongrass stalk, outer layer
    discarded, finely chopped
2 garlic cloves, chopped
1-inch/2.5-cm piece fresh
    gingerroot, grated
2 kaffir lime leaves, finely
    chopped (optional)
2 shallots, finely chopped
2 fresh red chiles, seeded
    and finely chopped
4 tbsp chopped fresh cilantro
3^1/4 oz/90 g/scant ^{3}/4 cup
    gluten-free all-purpose
    flour, plus extra for flouring
^{1}/2 tsp salt
corn oil, for cooking

chili dip

3 tbsp white distilled vinegar
    or rice wine vinegar
2 scallions, finely sliced
1 tbsp superfine sugar
2 fresh chiles, finely chopped
2 tbsp chopped fresh cilantro
pinch of salt

method

1 To make the chili dip, mix all the ingredients together in a small serving bowl and set aside.

2 Mix the bean curd with the lemongrass, garlic, gingerroot, lime leaves, if using, shallots, chiles, and cilantro in a mixing bowl. Stir in the flour and salt to make a coarse, sticky paste. Cover and let chill in the refrigerator for 1 hour to let the mixture firm up slightly.

3 Form the mixture into 8 large walnut-size balls and, using floured hands, flatten into circles. Heat enough oil to cover the bottom of a large, heavy-bottom skillet over medium heat. Cook the cakes in 2 batches, turning halfway through, for 4–6 minutes, or until golden brown. Drain on paper towels and serve warm with the chili dip.

spicy bean curd

ingredients

SERVES 4

marinade

75 ml/2^{1}/$_{2}$ fl oz vegetable
    stock
2 tsp cornstarch
2 tbsp soy sauce
1 tbsp superfine sugar
pinch of chile flakes

stir-fry

9 oz/250 g firm bean curd,
    rinsed and drained
    thoroughly and cut into
    ^{1}/$_{2}$-inch/1-cm cubes
4 tbsp peanut oil
1 tbsp grated fresh gingerroot
3 garlic cloves, crushed
4 scallions, sliced thinly
1 head of broccoli,
    cut into florets
1 carrot, cut into batons
1 yellow bell pepper,
    sliced thinly
9 oz/250 g/5 cups shiitake
    mushrooms, sliced thinly
steamed rice, to serve

method

1 Blend the vegetable stock, cornstarch, soy sauce, sugar, and chile flakes together in a large bowl. Add the bean curd and toss well to coat. Set aside to marinate for 20 minutes.

2 In a wok or large skillet, heat 2 tablespoons of the peanut oil and stir-fry the bean curd with its marinade until brown and crispy. Remove from the wok and set aside.

3 Heat the remaining 2 tablespoons of peanut oil in the wok and stir-fry the ginger, garlic, and scallions for 30 seconds. Add the broccoli, carrot, yellow bell pepper, and mushrooms to the wok and cook for 5–6 minutes. Return the bean curd to the wok and stir-fry to reheat. Serve immediately over steamed rice.

pasta, noodles & rice

Pasta, noodles, and rice are always popular and lend themselves perfectly to the vegetarian treatment. The scope for pasta sauces is endless, and here you will find a handful of really special recipes—Fusilli with Gorgonzola & Mushroom Sauce, for example, is rich, stylish, and full of flavor, while Pasta with Pesto is a classic, not to be missed. If you've never made your own pesto sauce before, you will be surprised at how easy it is—pick the basil at the last minute for the freshest flavor.

Noodles are wonderful for adding bulk to a stir-fry, but for a different way of serving them, try Sweet-&-Sour Vegetables on Noodle Pancakes, or cook them in stock with vegetables, an excellent recipe for a lowfat diet.

Most cultures throughout the world have a favorite rice dish, and in Italy this is risotto, made with a plump, short-grain rice that releases its starch on cooking to give a creamy result that works wonderfully with vegetables—try the Risotto Primavera, with fresh spring vegetables. Paella is the traditional Spanish rice dish—made with saffron to color it yellow, it really is the perfect sunshine food. If you like Asian cuisine, try Stir-fried Rice with Green Vegetables from Thailand or Vegetable Biryani, a classic dish from India. You'll never be short of inspiration!

vegetarian lasagna

ingredients

SERVES 4

olive oil, for brushing

2 eggplants, sliced

2 tbsp butter

1 garlic clove, finely chopped

4 zucchini, sliced

1 tbsp finely chopped fresh
flat-leaf parsley

1 tbsp finely chopped fresh
marjoram

8 oz/225 g mozzarella
cheese, grated

20 fl oz/625 ml/2^1/$_2$ cups
strained canned tomatoes

175 g/6 oz dried no-precook
lasagna

salt and pepper

béchamel sauce (see below)

2 oz/55 g^1/$_2$ cup freshly
grated Parmesan cheese

béchamel sauce

10 fl oz/300 ml/1^1/$_4$ cups milk

1 bay leaf

6 black peppercorns

slice of onion

mace blade

2 tbsp butter

3 tbsp all-purpose flour

salt and pepper

method

1 To make the béchamel sauce, pour the milk into a pan and add the bay leaf, peppercorns, onion, and mace. Heat to just below boiling point, then remove from the heat, cover, let infuse for 10 minutes, then strain. Melt the butter in a separate pan. Sprinkle in the flour and cook over low heat, stirring constantly, for 1 minute. Gradually stir in the milk, then bring to a boil and cook, stirring, until thickened and smooth. Season with salt and pepper.

2 Brush a grill pan with olive oil and heat until smoking. Add half the eggplant slices and cook over medium heat for 8 minutes, or until golden brown all over. Remove from the grill pan and drain on paper towels. Repeat with the remaining eggplant slices.

3 Melt the butter in a skillet and add the garlic, zucchini, parsley, and marjoram. Cook over medium heat, stirring frequently, for 5 minutes, or until the zucchini are golden brown all over. Remove and let drain on paper towels.

4 Layer the eggplant, zucchini, mozzarella, strained tomatoes, and lasagna in an ovenproof dish brushed with olive oil, seasoning as you go and finishing with a layer of lasagna. Pour over the béchamel sauce, making sure that all the pasta is covered. Sprinkle with Parmesan cheese and bake in a preheated oven, 400°F/200°C, for 30–40 minutes, or until golden brown. Serve at once.

fusilli with gorgonzola and mushroom sauce

ingredients

SERVES 4

12 oz/350 g dried fusilli

3 tbsp olive oil

12 oz/350 g wild mushrooms
or white mushrooms, sliced

1 garlic clove, finely chopped

14 fl oz/400 ml/1^{3}/$_{4}$ cups
heavy cream

9 oz/250 g Gorgonzola
cheese, crumbled

salt and pepper

2 tbsp chopped fresh
flat-leaf parsley, to garnish

method

1 Bring a large pan of lightly salted water to a boil. Add the pasta, return to a boil, and cook for 8–10 minutes, or until tender but still firm to the bite.

2 Meanwhile, heat the olive oil in a heavy-bottom pan. Add the mushrooms and cook over low heat, stirring frequently, for 5 minutes. Add the garlic and cook for an additional 2 minutes.

3 Add the cream, bring to a boil, and cook for 1 minute until slightly thickened. Stir in the cheese and cook over low heat until it has melted. Do not allow the sauce to boil once the cheese has been added. Season with salt and pepper and remove the pan from the heat.

4 Drain the pasta and tip it into the sauce. Toss well to coat, then serve immediately, garnished with the parsley.

chile broccoli pasta

ingredients

SERVES 4

8 oz/225 g dried penne or
    macaroni
8 oz/225 g broccoli, cut into
    florets
2 fl oz/50 ml/$\frac{1}{4}$ cup extra-
    virgin olive oil
2 large garlic cloves, chopped
2 fresh red chiles, seeded
    and diced
8 cherry tomatoes (optional)
fresh basil leaves, to garnish

method

1 Bring a large pan of salted boiling water to a boil. Add the pasta, return to a boil, and cook for 8–10 minutes until tender but still firm to the bite. Drain the pasta, refresh under cold running water, and drain again. Set aside.

2 Bring a separate pan of salted water to a boil, add the broccoli, and cook for 5 minutes. Drain, refresh under cold running water, and drain again.

3 Heat the oil, in the pan that the pasta was cooked in, over high heat. Add the garlic, chiles, and tomatoes, if using, and cook, stirring, for 1 minute.

4 Add the broccoli and mix well. Cook for 2 minutes, stirring, to heat through. Add the pasta and mix well again. Cook for an additional minute. Transfer the pasta to a large, warmed serving bowl and serve garnished with basil leaves.

pasta with pesto

ingredients

SERVES 4

1 lb/450 g dried tagliatelle
fresh basil sprigs, to garnish

pesto
2 garlic cloves
1 oz/25 g/$1/4$ cup pine nuts
salt
4 oz/115 g fresh basil leaves
2 oz/55 g/$1/2$ cup freshly
   grated Parmesan cheese
4 fl oz/125 ml/$1/2$ cup olive oil

method

1 To make the pesto, put the garlic, pine nuts, a large pinch of salt, and the basil into a mortar and pound to a paste with a pestle. Transfer to a bowl and gradually work in the Parmesan cheese with a wooden spoon, followed by the olive oil, to make a thick, creamy sauce. Taste and adjust the seasoning if necessary.

2 Alternatively, put the garlic, pine nuts, and a large pinch of salt into a food processor or blender and process briefly. Add the basil leaves and process to a paste. With the motor still running, gradually add the olive oil. Scrape into a bowl and beat in the Parmesan cheese.

3 Bring a large pan of lightly salted water to a boil. Add the pasta, return to a boil, and cook for 8–10 minutes, or until tender but still firm to the bite. Drain the pasta well, return to the pan, and toss with half the pesto, then divide among warmed serving plates and top with the remaining pesto. Garnish with basil sprigs and serve immediately.

macaroni & cheese

ingredients

SERVES 4

8 oz/225 g macaroni

1 egg, beaten

4^1/$_2$ oz/125 g/1^1/$_4$ cups sharp
    Cheddar cheese, grated

1 tbsp wholegrain mustard

2 tbsp chopped fresh chives

20 fl oz/625 ml/2^1/$_2$ cups
    béchamel sauce
    (see page 104)

salt and pepper

4 tomatoes, sliced

4^1/$_2$ oz/125 g/1^1/$_4$ cups Red
    Leicester cheese, grated

2^1/$_4$ oz/60 g/generous ^{1}/$_2$ cup
    bleu cheese, grated

2 tbsp sunflower seeds

snipped fresh chives,
    to garnish

method

1 Bring a large pan of lightly salted water to a boil and cook the macaroni for 8–10 minutes, or until just tender. Drain well and place in an ovenproof dish.

2 Stir the beaten egg, Cheddar cheese, mustard, and chives into the béchamel sauce and season with salt and pepper. Spoon the mixture over the macaroni, making sure it is well covered. Top with a layer of the sliced tomatoes.

3 Sprinkle the Red Leicester cheese, bleu cheese, and sunflower seeds over the top. Place on a cookie sheet and bake in a preheated oven, 375°F/190°C, for 25–30 minutes, or until bubbling and golden. Garnish with snipped fresh chives and serve at once.

creamy spinach & mushroom pasta

ingredients

SERVES 4

10^1/$_2$ oz/300 g dried
    gluten-free penne or
    pasta of your choice
2 tbsp olive oil
9 oz/250 g mushrooms, sliced
1 tsp dried oregano
9 fl oz/275 ml/scant 1^1/$_4$ cups
    vegetable stock
1 tbsp lemon juice
6 tbsp cream cheese
7 oz/200 g frozen spinach
    leaves
salt and pepper

method

1 Cook the pasta in a large pan of lightly salted boiling water, according to the package instructions. Drain, reserving 6 fl oz/175 ml/ 3/4 cup of the cooking liquid.

2 Meanwhile, heat the oil in a large, heavy-bottom skillet over medium heat, add the mushrooms, and cook, stirring frequently, for 8 minutes, or until almost crisp. Stir in the oregano, stock, and lemon juice and cook for 10–12 minutes, or until the sauce is reduced by half.

3 Stir in the cream cheese and spinach and cook over medium-low heat for 3–5 minutes. Add the reserved cooking liquid, then the cooked pasta. Stir well, season with salt and pepper, and heat through gently before serving.

artichoke & olive spaghetti

ingredients

SERVES 4

2 tbsp olive oil

1 large red onion, chopped

2 garlic cloves, crushed

1 tbsp lemon juice

4 baby eggplants, quartered

20 fl oz/625 ml/2$\frac{1}{2}$ cups
    strained tomatoes

salt and pepper

2 tsp superfine sugar

2 tbsp tomato paste

14 oz/400 g canned artichoke
    hearts, drained and halved

4$\frac{1}{2}$ oz/125 g/$\frac{2}{3}$ cup
    pitted black olives

12 oz/350 g whole wheat
    dried spaghetti

fresh basil sprigs, to garnish

olive bread, to serve

method

1 Heat 1 tablespoon of the oil in a large skillet and gently cook the onion, garlic, lemon juice, and eggplants for 4–5 minutes, or until lightly browned.

2 Pour in the strained tomatoes, season with salt and pepper, and add the sugar and tomato paste. Bring to a boil, reduce the heat, and let simmer for 20 minutes. Gently stir in the artichoke halves and olives, and cook for 5 minutes.

3 Meanwhile, bring a large, heavy-bottom pan of lightly salted water to a boil. Add the spaghetti, return to a boil, and cook for 8–10 minutes, or until just tender, but still firm to the bite. Drain well, toss in the remaining olive oil, and season with salt and pepper.

4 Transfer the spaghetti to a warmed serving bowl and top with the vegetable sauce. Garnish with the basil sprigs and serve with olive bread.

radiatore with pumpkin sauce

ingredients

SERVES 4

4 tbsp unsalted butter

4 oz/115 g white onions or
  shallots, very finely chopped

salt and pepper

1 lb 12 oz/800 g pumpkin,
  unprepared weight

pinch of freshly grated nutmeg

12 oz/350 g dried radiatore

7 fl oz/200 ml/generous
  ³/₄ cup light cream

4 tbsp freshly grated
  Parmesan cheese,
  plus extra to serve

2 tbsp chopped fresh
  flat-leaf parsley, plus extra
  to garnish

method

1 Melt the butter in a heavy-bottom pan over low heat. Add the onions, sprinkle with a little salt, cover, and cook, stirring frequently, for 25–30 minutes.

2 Scoop out and discard the seeds from the pumpkin. Peel and finely chop the flesh. Tip the pumpkin into the pan and season with nutmeg. Cover and cook over low heat, stirring occasionally, for 45 minutes.

3 Meanwhile, bring a large pan of lightly salted water to a boil. Add the pasta, return to a boil, and cook for 8–10 minutes, or until tender but still firm to the bite. Drain thoroughly, reserving about 5 fl oz/150 ml/²/₃ cup of the cooking liquid.

4 Stir the cream, grated Parmesan cheese, and parsley into the pumpkin sauce and season with salt and pepper. If the mixture seems a little too thick, add some or all of the reserved cooking liquid and stir. Tip in the pasta and toss for 1 minute. Serve immediately, garnished with chopped parsley, with extra Parmesan cheese for sprinkling.

crisp noodle & vegetable stir-fry

ingredients

SERVES 4

peanut or sunflower oil,
   for deep-frying

4 oz/115 g rice vermicelli,
   broken into 3-inch/7.5-cm
   lengths

4 oz/115 g green beans,
   cut into short lengths

2 carrots, cut into thin sticks

2 zucchini, cut into thin sticks

4 oz/115 g shiitake
   mushrooms, sliced

1-inch/2.5-cm piece fresh
   gingerroot, shredded

$1/2$ small head Napa cabbage,
   shredded

4 scallions, shredded

3 oz/85 g/$1/2$ cup bean
   sprouts

2 tbsp dark soy sauce

2 tbsp Chinese rice wine

large pinch of sugar

2 tbsp coarsely chopped
   fresh cilantro

method

1 Half-fill a wok or deep, heavy-bottom skillet with oil. Heat to 350–375°F/180–190°C, or until a cube of bread browns in 30 seconds.

2 Add the noodles, in batches, and cook for $1^1/_2$–2 minutes, or until crisp and puffed up. Remove and drain on paper towels. Pour off all but 2 tablespoons of oil from the wok.

3 Heat the remaining oil over high heat. Add the green beans and stir-fry for 2 minutes. Add the carrot and zucchini sticks, sliced mushrooms, and gingerroot and stir-fry for an additional 2 minutes.

4 Add the shredded Napa cabbage, scallions, and bean sprouts and stir-fry for an additional 1 minute. Add the soy sauce, rice wine, and sugar and cook, stirring constantly, for 1 minute.

5 Add the chopped cilantro and toss well. Serve immediately, with the noodles.

chinese vegetables & bean sprouts with noodles

ingredients

SERVES 4

40 fl oz/1.25 liters/5 cups
   vegetable stock
1 garlic clove, crushed
$1/2$-inch/1-cm piece fresh
   gingerroot, finely chopped
8 oz/225 g dried medium
   egg noodles
1 red bell pepper, seeded
   and sliced
3 oz/85 g/$3/4$ cup frozen peas
4 oz/115 g broccoli florets
3 oz/85 g shiitake
   mushrooms, sliced
2 tbsp sesame seeds
8 oz/225 g canned water
   chestnuts, drained
   and halved
8 oz/225 g canned bamboo
   shoots, drained
10 oz/280 g Napa cabbage,
   sliced
5 oz/140 g/scant 1 cup
   bean sprouts
3 scallions, sliced
1 tbsp dark soy sauce
pepper

method

1 Bring the stock, garlic, and gingerroot to a boil in a large pan. Stir in the noodles, red bell pepper, peas, broccoli, and mushrooms and return to a boil. Reduce the heat, cover, and let simmer for 5–6 minutes, or until the noodles are tender.

2 Meanwhile, preheat the broiler to medium. Spread the sesame seeds out in a single layer on a cookie sheet and toast under the preheated broiler, turning to brown evenly— watch constantly because they brown very quickly. Tip the sesame seeds into a small dish and set aside.

3 Once the noodles are tender, add the water chestnuts, bamboo shoots, Napa cabbage, bean sprouts, and scallions to the pan. Return the stock to a boil, stir to mix the ingredients, and let simmer for an additional 2–3 minutes to heat through thoroughly.

4 Carefully drain off 10 fl oz/300 ml/1$1/4$ cups of the stock into a small heatproof pitcher and set aside. Drain and discard any remaining stock and turn the noodles and vegetables into a warmed serving dish. Quickly mix the soy sauce with the reserved stock and pour over the noodles and vegetables. Season with pepper and serve at once.

sweet-&-sour vegetables on noodle pancakes

ingredients

SERVES 4

4 oz/115 g dried thin
   cellophane noodles

6 eggs

4 scallions, sliced diagonally

salt and pepper

2^1/$_2$ tbsp peanut or corn oil

2 lb/900 g selection of
   vegetables, such as carrots,
   baby corn, cauliflower,
   broccoli, snow peas, and
   onions, peeled as
   necessary and chopped
   into same-size pieces

3^1/$_2$ oz/100 g canned bamboo
   shoots, drained

7 oz/200 g/scant 1 cup
   bottled sweet-and-sour
   sauce

method

1 Soak the noodles in enough lukewarm water to cover and let stand for 20 minutes, until soft. Alternatively, cook according to the package instructions. Drain them well and use scissors to cut into 3-inch/7.5-cm pieces, then set aside.

2 Beat the eggs, then stir in the noodles, the scallions, salt, and pepper. Heat an 8-inch/20-cm skillet over high heat. Add 1 tablespoon oil and swirl it round. Pour in a fourth of the egg mixture and tilt the skillet so it covers the bottom. Lower the heat to medium and cook for 1 minute, or until the thin pancake is set. Flip it over, adding a little extra oil, if necessary, and cook the other side until golden. Keep warm in a low oven while you make 3 more pancakes.

3 After you've made 4 pancakes, heat a wok or large, heavy-bottom skillet over high heat. Add 1^1/$_2$ tablespoons oil and heat until it shimmers. Add the thickest vegetables, such as carrots, first and stir-fry for 30 seconds. Gradually add the remaining vegetables and bamboo shoots. Stir in the sauce and stir-fry until all the vegetables are tender and the sauce is hot. Spoon the vegetables and sauce over the pancakes.

crunchy walnut risotto

ingredients

SERVES 4

1 tbsp olive oil

$2^1/_2$ oz/70 g butter

1 small onion,
   finely chopped

10 oz/280 g/$1^1/_2$ cups
   Arborio rice

40 fl oz/1.25 liters/5 cups
   simmering vegetable
   stock

salt and pepper

4 oz/115 g/1 cup
   walnut halves

3 oz/85 g/$^3/_4$ cup freshly
   grated Parmesan or Grana
   Padano cheese

2 oz/55 g/$^1/_4$ cup Mascarpone
   cheese

2 oz/55 g Gorgonzola cheese,
   diced

method

1 Heat the oil with 2 tablespoons of the butter in a deep pan over medium heat until the butter has melted. Add the onion and cook, stirring occasionally, for 5–7 minutes, or until soft and starting to turn golden. Do not brown.

2 Reduce the heat, add the rice, and mix to coat in oil and butter. Cook, stirring constantly, for 2–3 minutes, or until the grains are translucent.

3 Gradually add the hot stock, a ladleful at a time. Stir constantly and add more liquid as the rice absorbs each addition. Increase the heat to medium so that the liquid bubbles. Cook for 20 minutes, or until all the liquid is absorbed and the rice is creamy. Season with salt and pepper.

4 Melt 2 tablespoons of the remaining butter in a skillet over medium heat. Add the walnuts and toss for 2–3 minutes, or until just starting to brown.

5 Remove the risotto from the heat and add the remaining butter. Mix well, then stir in the Parmesan, Mascarpone, and Gorgonzola until they melt, along with most of the walnuts. Spoon the risotto onto warmed plates, sprinkle with the remaining walnuts, and serve.

wild mushroom risotto

ingredients

SERVES 6

2 oz/55 g/^{1}/$_2$ cup dried porcini or morel mushrooms

about 1 lb 2 oz/500 g mixed fresh wild mushrooms, such as porcini, horse mushrooms, and chanterelles, halved if large

4 tbsp olive oil

3–4 garlic cloves, finely chopped

2 oz/55 g butter

1 onion, finely chopped

12 oz/350 g/1^3/$_4$ cups Arborio rice

2 fl oz/50 ml/^{1}/$_4$ cup dry white vermouth

40/1.25 liters/5 cups simmering vegetable stock

salt and pepper

4 oz/115 g/1 cup freshly grated Parmesan cheese

4 tbsp chopped fresh flat-leaf parsley

method

1 Place the dried mushrooms in a heatproof bowl and add boiling water to cover. Set aside to soak for 30 minutes, then carefully lift out and pat dry. Strain the soaking liquid through a strainer lined with paper towels and set aside.

2 Trim the fresh mushrooms and gently brush clean. Heat 3 tablespoons of the oil in a large skillet. Add the fresh mushrooms and stir-fry for 1–2 minutes. Add the garlic and the soaked mushrooms and cook, stirring frequently, for 2 minutes. Transfer to a plate.

3 Heat the remaining oil and half the butter in a pan. Add the onion and cook over medium heat, stirring, until softened. Reduce the heat, add the rice, and cook, stirring, until the grains are translucent. Add the vermouth and cook, stirring, for 1 minute until reduced.

4 Gradually add the hot stock, a ladleful at a time. Stir constantly and add more liquid as the rice absorbs each addition. Increase the heat to medium so that the liquid bubbles. Cook for 20 minutes, or until all the liquid is absorbed and the rice is creamy.

5 Add half the reserved mushroom soaking liquid and stir in the mushrooms. Season and add more mushroom liquid, if necessary. Remove from the heat and stir in the remaining butter, the grated Parmesan, and chopped parsley. Serve at once.

risotto primavera

ingredients

SERVES 6–8

8 oz/225 g fresh thin
  asparagus spears
4 tbsp olive oil
6 oz/175 g young green
  beans, cut into 1-inch/
  2.5-cm lengths
6 oz/175 g young zucchini,
  quartered and cut into
  1-inch/2.5-cm lengths
8 oz/225 g/generous
  1^1/$_2$ cups shelled
  fresh peas
1 onion, finely chopped
1–2 garlic cloves, finely
  chopped
12 oz/350 g/1^3/$_4$ cups
  Arborio rice
52 fl oz/1.6 liters/generous
  6^1/$_3$ cups simmering
  vegetable stock
4 scallions, cut into
  1-inch/2.5-cm lengths
salt and pepper
2 oz/55 g butter
4 oz/115 g/1 cup freshly
  grated Parmesan cheese
2 tbsp snipped fresh chives
2 tbsp shredded fresh basil
scallions, to garnish (optional)

method

1 Trim the woody ends of the asparagus and cut off the tips. Cut the stems into 1-inch/2.5-cm pieces and set aside with the tips.

2 Heat 2 tablespoons of the oil in a large skillet over high heat until very hot. Add the asparagus, beans, zucchini, and peas and stir-fry for 3–4 minutes until they are bright green and just starting to soften. Set aside.

3 Heat the remaining oil in a large, heavy-bottom pan over medium heat. Add the onion and cook, stirring occasionally, for 3 minutes, or until it starts to soften. Stir in the garlic and cook, while stirring, for 30 seconds. Reduce the heat, add the rice, and mix to coat in oil. Cook, stirring constantly, for 2–3 minutes, or until the grains are translucent.

4 Gradually add the hot stock, a ladleful at a time. Stir constantly and add more liquid as the rice absorbs each addition. Increase the heat to medium so that the liquid bubbles. Cook for 20 minutes, or until all but 2 tablespoons of the liquid is absorbed and the rice is creamy.

5 Stir in the stir-fried vegetables, onion mixture, and scallions with the remaining stock. Cook for 2 minutes, stirring frequently, then season with salt and pepper. Stir in the butter, Parmesan, chives, and basil. Remove the pan from the heat and serve the risotto at once, garnished with scallions, if liked.

spiced risotto cakes

ingredients

SERVES 3

3 oz/85 g onion, finely
    chopped

3 oz/85 g leek, finely chopped

1 oz/25g/^{1}/$_8$ cup Arborio rice

18 fl oz/550 ml/scant
    2^1/$_2$ cups vegetable stock

3 oz/85 g/scant ^{1}/$_2$ cup grated
    zucchini

1 tbsp fresh basil, chopped

1 oz/25g/^{1}/$_2$ cup fresh whole
    wheat bread crumbs

vegetable oil spray

radicchio leaves, to serve

filling

1^3/$_4$ oz/50 g/scant ^{1}/$_4$ cup
    cream cheese

1^3/$_4$ oz/50 g mango, diced

1 tsp finely grated lime rind

1 tsp lime juice

pinch of cayenne pepper

method

1 Heat a large, nonstick pan over high heat, add the onion and leek, and cook, stirring constantly, for 2–3 minutes, or until softened but not colored.

2 Add the rice and stock, bring to a boil, then continue to boil, stirring constantly, for 2 minutes. Reduce the heat and cook for an additional 15 minutes, stirring every 2–3 minutes. When the rice is nearly cooked and has absorbed all the stock, stir in the zucchini and basil and cook, continuing to stir, over high heat for an additional 5–10 minutes or until the mixture is sticky and dry. Turn out onto a plate and let cool.

3 Meanwhile, to make the filling, mix the cream cheese, mango, lime rind and juice, and cayenne together in a bowl.

4 Divide the cooled rice mixture into 3 and form into cakes. Make an indentation in the center of each cake and fill with 1 tbsp of the filling. Mold the sides up and over to seal in the filling, then reshape with a palette knife. Coat each cake with bread crumbs and arrange on a nonstick cookie sheet. Spray each cake lightly with oil and bake in a preheated oven, 400°F/200°C, for 15–20 minutes, or until a light golden brown color. Serve with radicchio leaves.

stir-fried rice with green vegetables

ingredients

SERVES 4

8 oz/225 g/generous 1 cup jasmine rice

2 tbsp vegetable or peanut oil

1 tbsp green curry paste

6 scallions, sliced

2 garlic cloves, crushed

1 zucchini, cut into thin sticks

4 oz green beans

6 oz asparagus, trimmed

3–4 fresh Thai basil leaves

method

1 Cook the rice in lightly salted boiling water for 12–15 minutes, drain well, then cool thoroughly and chill overnight.

2 Heat the oil in a wok and stir-fry the curry paste for 1 minute. Add the scallions and garlic and stir-fry for 1 minute.

3 Add the zucchini, beans, and asparagus, and stir-fry for 3–4 minutes, until just tender. Break up the rice and add it to the wok. Cook, stirring constantly for 2–3 minutes, until the rice is hot. Stir in the basil leaves. Serve hot.

brown rice vegetable pilaf

ingredients

SERVES 4

4 tbsp vegetable oil

1 red onion, finely chopped

2 tender celery stalks, leaves
included, quartered
lengthwise, and diced

2 carrots, coarsely grated

1 fresh green chile, seeded
and finely chopped

3 scallions, green part
included, finely chopped

$1^1/_2$ oz/40 g/generous $^1/_4$ cup
whole almonds, sliced
lengthwise

12 oz/350 g/$1^3/_4$ cups cooked
brown basmati rice

$5^1/_2$ oz/150 g/$^3/_4$ cup cooked
split red lentils

6 fl oz/175 ml/$^3/_4$ cup
vegetable stock

5 tbsp fresh orange juice

salt and pepper

fresh celery leaves, to garnish

method

1 Heat 2 tablespoons of the oil, in a high-sided skillet with a lid, over medium heat. Add the onion. Cook for 5 minutes, or until softened.

2 Add the celery, carrots, chile, scallions, and almonds. Stir-fry for 2 minutes, or until the vegetables are al dente but still brightly colored. Transfer to a bowl and set aside until required.

3 Add the remaining oil to the skillet. Stir in the rice and lentils. Cook over medium-high heat, stirring, for 1–2 minutes, or until heated through. Reduce the heat. Stir in the stock and orange juice. Season with salt and pepper.

4 Return the vegetables to the skillet. Toss with the rice for a few minutes until heated through. Transfer to a warmed dish, garnish with celery leaves, and serve.

artichoke paella

ingredients

SERVES 4–6

$^1/_2$ tsp saffron threads

2 tbsp hot water

3 tbsp olive oil

1 large onion, chopped

1 zucchini, coarsely chopped

2 garlic cloves, crushed

$^1/_4$ tsp cayenne pepper

8 oz/225 g tomatoes, peeled
    and cut into wedges

15 oz/425 g canned
    chickpeas, drained

15 oz/425 g canned
    artichokes hearts, drained
    and coarsely sliced

12 oz/350 g/generous
    1$^1/_2$ cups medium-grain
    paella rice

42 fl oz/1.3 liters/5$^1/_2$ cups
    simmering vegetable stock

5$^1/_2$ oz/150 g green beans,
    blanched

salt and pepper

1 lemon, cut into wedges,
    to serve

method

1 Put the saffron threads and water in a small bowl and let infuse for a few minutes.

2 Meanwhile, heat the oil in a paella pan and cook the onion and zucchini over medium heat, stirring, for 2–3 minutes, or until softened. Add the garlic, cayenne pepper, and saffron and its soaking liquid and cook, stirring constantly, for 1 minute. Add the tomato wedges, chickpeas, and artichokes and cook, stirring, for an additional 2 minutes.

3 Add the rice and cook, stirring constantly, for 1 minute, or until the rice is glossy and coated. Pour in most of the hot stock and bring to a boil, then let simmer, uncovered, for 10 minutes. Do not stir during cooking, but shake the pan once or twice. Add the green beans and season. Shake the pan and cook for an additional 10–15 minutes, or until the rice grains are plump and cooked. If the liquid is absorbed too quickly, pour in a little more hot stock, then shake the pan to spread the liquid through the paella.

4 When all the liquid has been absorbed and you detect a faint toasty aroma coming from the rice, remove from the heat immediately to prevent burning. Cover the pan with a clean dish towel or foil and let stand for 5 minutes. Serve direct from the pan with the lemon wedges to squeeze over the rice.

vegetarian paella

ingredients

SERVES 4–6

$1/2$ tsp saffron threads

2 tbsp hot water

6 tbsp olive oil

1 Spanish onion, sliced

3 garlic cloves, minced

1 red bell pepper, seeded and
sliced

1 orange bell pepper, seeded
and sliced

1 large eggplant, cubed

7 oz/200 g/1 cup medium-
grain paella rice

20 fl oz/625 ml/$2^{1}/2$ cups
vegetable stock

1 lb/450 g tomatoes, peeled
and chopped

salt and pepper

4 oz/115 g mushrooms, sliced

4 oz/115 g green beans, halved

14 oz/400 g canned
pinto beans

method

1 Put the saffron threads and water in a small bowl or cup and let infuse for a few minutes.

2 Meanwhile, heat the oil in a paella pan or wide, shallow skillet and cook the onion over medium heat, stirring, for 2–3 minutes, or until softened. Add the garlic, bell peppers, and eggplant and cook, stirring frequently, for 5 minutes.

3 Add the rice and cook, stirring constantly, for 1 minute, or until glossy and coated. Pour in the stock and add the tomatoes, saffron and its soaking water, salt, and pepper. Bring to a boil, then reduce the heat and let simmer, shaking the skillet frequently and stirring occasionally, for 15 minutes.

4 Stir in the mushrooms, green beans, and pinto beans with their can juices. Cook for an additional 10 minutes, then serve immediately.

paella de verduras

ingredients

SERVES 4–6

$^1/_2$ tsp saffron threads

2 tbsp hot water

3 tbsp olive oil

1 large onion, chopped

2 garlic cloves, crushed

1 tsp paprika

8 oz/225 g tomatoes, peeled
and cut into wedges

1 red bell pepper, halved and
seeded, then broiled,
peeled, and sliced

1 green bell pepper, halved
and seeded, then broiled,
peeled, and sliced

15 oz/425 g canned
chickpeas, drained

12 oz/350 g/generous
$1^1/_2$ cups medium-grain
paella rice

42 fl oz/1.3 liters/$5^1/_2$ cups
simmering vegetable stock

2 oz/55 g/$^3/_8$ cup shelled peas

$5^1/_2$ oz/150 g fresh asparagus
spears, blanched

salt and pepper

1 tbsp chopped fresh flat-leaf
parsley, plus extra
to garnish

1 lemon, cut into wedges,
to serve

method

1 Put the saffron threads and water in a small bowl and let infuse for a few minutes.

2 Meanwhile, heat the oil in a paella pan and cook the onion over medium heat, stirring, for 2–3 minutes, or until softened. Add the garlic, paprika, and saffron and its soaking liquid and cook, stirring, for 1 minute. Add the tomatoes, bell peppers, and chickpeas and cook, stirring, for an additional 2 minutes.

3 Add the rice and cook, stirring constantly, for 1 minute or until glossy and coated. Pour in most of the hot stock and bring to a boil. Reduce the heat and let simmer, uncovered, for 10 minutes. Do not stir during cooking, but shake the pan once or twice. Add the peas, asparagus, and parsley and season with salt and pepper. Shake the pan and cook for an additional 10–15 minutes, or until the rice grains are plump and cooked. Pour in a little more hot stock if necessary, then shake the pan to spread the liquid through the paella.

4 When all the liquid has been absorbed and you detect a faint toasty aroma coming from the rice, remove from the heat immediately to prevent burning. Cover the pan with a clean dish towel or foil and let stand for 5 minutes. Sprinkle over chopped parsley to garnish and serve direct from the pan with the lemon wedges for squeezing over the rice.

vegetable biryani

ingredients

SERVES 4

2 tbsp vegetable oil

3 whole cloves

3 cardamom pods, cracked

1 onion, chopped

4 oz/115 g carrots, chopped

2–3 garlic cloves, crushed

1–2 fresh red chiles, seeded
and chopped

1-inch/2.5-cm piece fresh
gingerroot, grated

4 oz/115 g cauliflower, broken
into small florets

6 oz/175 g broccoli, broken
into small florets

4 oz/115 g green beans,
chopped

14 oz/400 g canned chopped
tomatoes

5 fl oz/150 ml/²/₃ cup
vegetable stock

salt and pepper

4 oz/115 g okra, sliced

1 tbsp chopped fresh cilantro,
plus extra sprigs to garnish

4 oz/115 g/generous ¹/₄ cup
brown basmati rice

few saffron threads (optional)

grated lime rind, to garnish

method

1 Heat the oil in a large pan over low heat, add the spices, onion, carrots, garlic, chiles, and gingerroot and cook, stirring frequently, for 5 minutes.

2 Add the cauliflower, broccoli, and green beans and cook, stirring frequently, for 5 minutes. Stir in the tomatoes, stock, salt, and pepper and bring to a boil. Reduce the heat, cover, and let simmer for 10 minutes.

3 Add the okra and cook for an additional 8–10 minutes, or until the vegetables are tender. Stir in the cilantro. Strain off any excess liquid and keep warm.

4 Meanwhile, cook the rice with the saffron in a pan of lightly salted boiling water for 25 minutes, or until tender. Drain and keep warm.

5 Layer the vegetables and cooked rice in a deep dish or ovenproof bowl, packing the layers down firmly. Let stand for about 5 minutes, then invert on to a warmed serving dish and serve, garnished with grated lime rind and cilantro sprigs, with the reserved liquid.

stuffed red bell peppers with basil

ingredients

SERVES 4

5 oz/140 g/³/₄ cup long-grain
white or brown rice

4 large red bell peppers

2 tbsp olive oil

1 garlic clove, chopped

4 shallots, chopped

1 celery stalk, chopped

3 tbsp chopped
toasted walnuts

2 tomatoes, peeled
and chopped

1 tbsp lemon juice

1³/₄ oz/50 g/¹/₃ cup raisins

4 tbsp freshly grated
Cheddar cheese

2 tbsp chopped fresh basil

salt and pepper

fresh basil sprigs, to garnish

lemon wedges, to serve

method

1 Cook the rice in a pan of lightly salted boiling water for 20 minutes, if using white rice, or 35 minutes, if using brown. Drain, rinse under cold running water, then drain again.

2 Using a sharp knife, cut the tops off the bell peppers and set aside. Remove the seeds and white cores, then blanch the bell peppers and reserved tops in boiling water for 2 minutes. Remove from the heat and drain well. Heat half the oil in a large skillet. Add the garlic and shallots and cook, stirring, for 3 minutes. Add the celery, walnuts, tomatoes, lemon juice, and raisins and cook for an additional 5 minutes. Remove from the heat and stir in the cheese, chopped basil, salt and pepper.

3 Stuff the bell peppers with the rice mixture and arrange them in a baking dish. Place the tops on the bell peppers, drizzle over the remaining oil, loosely cover with foil, and bake in a preheated oven, 350°F/180°C, for 45 minutes. Remove from the oven, then garnish with basil sprigs and serve with lemon wedges.

vegetables
& salads

Vegetables are an essential part of any diet and there are endless ways of using them to add variety and interest. Potatoes are very homely and comforting, and marry well with cheese—Potato & Cheese Gratin and Potato-topped Vegetables, served golden and bubbling from the oven, are both absolutely gorgeous, while Stuffed Baked Potatoes make a simple, inexpensive midweek family dish.

There are some great ideas in this section for entertaining. Mushroom Stroganoff is rich and creamy—use a good selection of mushrooms for the best effect. Cherry Tomato Clafoutis and Potato, Fontina & Rosemary Tart, and Roasted Squash Wedges, served with an unusual three-grain risotto mix, are bound to impress, too.

To encourage anyone who thinks they don't like vegetables, try serving some extra special side dishes. Roasted Garlic Creamed Potatoes turn what can be a rather bland offering into a taste sensation; Stir-fried Broccoli is quite fabulous with a light coating of gingerroot and chili sauce; and Brussels Sprouts with Chestnuts and Roasted Onions are perfect to accompany a nut roast.

Salad vegetables are a great source of vitamins, and avocados are a highly nutritious superfood for vegetarians. Put the two together in an Avocado Salad with Lime Dressing—just heaven!

potato & cheese gratin

ingredients

SERVES 4-6

2 lb/900 g waxy potatoes,
   peeled and thinly sliced
1 large garlic clove, halved
butter, for greasing and
   dotting over the top
8 fl oz/225 ml/1 cup heavy
   cream
freshly grated nutmeg
salt and pepper
6 oz/175 g Gruyère cheese,
   finely grated

method

1 Put the potato slices in a bowl, cover with cold water and let stand for 5 minutes, then drain well.

2 Meanwhile, rub the bottom and sides of an oval gratin or ovenproof dish with the cut sides of the garlic halves, pressing down firmly to impart the flavor. Lightly grease the sides of the dish with butter.

3 Place the potatoes in a bowl with the cream and season with freshly grated nutmeg, salt, and pepper. Use your hands to mix everything together, then transfer the potatoes to the gratin dish and pour over any cream remaining in the bowl.

4 Sprinkle the cheese over the top and dot with butter. Place the gratin dish on a cookie sheet and bake in a preheated oven, 375°F/190°C, for 60–80 minutes, or until the potatoes are tender when pierced with a skewer and the top is golden and bubbling. Let stand for about 2 minutes, then serve straight from the gratin dish.

potato, fontina & rosemary tart

ingredients

SERVES 4

1 quantity puff pastry

all-purpose flour, for dusting

filling

3–4 waxy potatoes

10$\frac{1}{2}$ oz/300 g fontina
     cheese, cut into cubes

1 red onion, thinly sliced

3 large fresh rosemary sprigs

2 tbsp olive oil

salt and pepper

1 egg yolk

method

1 Roll out the dough on a lightly floured counter into a circle about 10 inches/25 cm in diameter and put on a cookie sheet.

2 Slice the potatoes as thinly as possible so that they are almost transparent—use a mandolin if you have one. Arrange the potato slices in a spiral, overlapping the slices to cover the pastry, leaving a 3/4-inch/2-cm margin around the edge.

3 Arrange the cheese and onion over the potatoes, sprinkle with the rosemary, and drizzle over the oil. Season to taste with salt and pepper and brush the edges with the egg yolk to glaze.

4 Bake in a preheated oven, 375°F/190°C, for 25 minutes, or until the potatoes are tender and the pastry is brown and crisp. Serve hot.

potato-topped vegetables

ingredients

SERVES 4

1 carrot, diced

6 oz/175 g cauliflower florets

6 oz/175 g broccoli florets

1 fennel bulb, sliced

$2^3/_4$ oz/75 g green beans,
   halved

2 tbsp butter

$2^1/_2$ tbsp all-purpose flour

5 fl oz/150 ml/$^2/_3$ cup
   vegetable stock

5 fl oz/150 ml/$^2/_3$ cup
   dry white wine

5 fl oz/150 ml/$^2/_3$ cup milk

6 oz/175 g cremini
   mushrooms, cut into
   fourths

2 tbsp chopped fresh sage

salt and pepper

topping

2 lb/990 g/generous 5 cups
   diced mealy potatoes

2 tbsp butter

4 tbsp plain yogurt

$2^1/_2$ oz/75 g/1 cup freshly
   grated Parmesan cheese

1 tsp fennel seeds

method

1 Cook the carrot, cauliflower, broccoli, fennel, and beans in a large pan of boiling water for 10 minutes, until just tender. Drain the vegetables thoroughly and set aside.

2 Melt the butter in a pan. Stir in the flour and cook for 1 minute. Remove from the heat and stir in the stock, wine, and milk. Return to the heat and bring to a boil, stirring until thickened. Stir in the reserved vegetables, mushrooms, sage and season with salt and pepper.

3 Meanwhile, make the topping. Cook the diced potatoes in a pan of boiling water for 10–15 minutes. Drain and mash with the butter, yogurt, and half the Parmesan cheese. Stir in the fennel seeds.

4 Spoon the vegetable mixture into a 32-fl oz/ 1-liter/4-cup pie dish. Spoon the potato over the top and sprinkle with the remaining cheese. Cook in a preheated oven, 375°F/ 190°C, for 30–35 minutes, until golden.

stuffed baked potatoes

ingredients

SERVES 4

2 lb/900 g baking potatoes,
  scrubbed
2 tbsp vegetable oil
1 tsp coarse sea salt
4 oz/115 g/$^1/_2$ cup butter
1 small onion, chopped
salt and pepper
4 oz/115 g/1 cup grated
  Cheddar cheese or
  crumbled bleu cheese
snipped fresh chives,
  to garnish

optional

4 tbsp canned, drained
  corn kernels
4 tbsp cooked mushrooms,
  zucchini, or bell peppers

method

1 Prick the potatoes in several places with a fork and put on a cookie sheet. Brush with the oil and sprinkle with the salt. Bake in a preheated oven, 375°F/190°C, for 1 hour, or until the skins are crispy and the insides are soft when pierced with a fork.

2 Meanwhile, melt 1 tablespoon of the butter in a small skillet over medium-low heat. Add the onion and cook, stirring occasionally, for 8–10 minutes until soft and golden. Set aside.

3 Cut the potatoes in half lengthwise. Scoop the flesh into a large bowl, leaving the skins intact. Set aside the skins. Increase the oven temperature to 400°F/200°C.

4 Coarsely mash the potato flesh and mix in the onion and remaining butter. Add salt and pepper to taste and stir in any of the optional ingredients. Spoon the mixture back into the reserved potato skins. Top with the cheese.

5 Cook the filled potato skins in the oven for 10 minutes, or until the cheese has melted and is beginning to brown. Garnish with chives and serve immediately.

roasted ratatouille & potato wedges

ingredients

SERVES 4

$10^1/_2$ oz/300 g potatoes in
their skins, scrubbed

7 oz/200 g eggplant, cut into
$^1/_2$-inch/1-cm wedges

$4^1/_2$ oz/125 g red onion cut
into $^1/_4$-inch/5-mm slices

7 oz/200 g seeded mixed bell
peppers, sliced into
$^1/_2$-inch/1-cm strips

6 oz/175 g zucchini, cut in
half lengthwise, then into
$^1/_2$-inch/1-cm slices

$4^1/_2$ oz/125 g cherry tomatoes

$3^1/_4$ oz/90 g lowfat cream
cheese

1 tsp runny honey

pinch of smoked paprika

1 tsp chopped fresh parsley

marinade

1 tsp vegetable oil

1 tbsp lemon juice

4 tbsp white wine

1 tsp sugar

2 tbsp chopped fresh basil

1 tsp fresh rosemary

1 tbsp fresh lemon thyme

$^1/_4$ tsp smoked paprika

method

1 Bake the potatoes in a preheated oven, 400°F/200°C, for 30 minutes, then remove and cut into wedges—the flesh should not be completely cooked.

2 To make the marinade, finely chop the rosemary and lemon thyme, then place all the ingredients in a bowl and blend with a hand-held electric blender until smooth, or use a food processor.

3 Put the potato wedges into a large bowl with the eggplant, onion, bell peppers, and zucchini, then pour over the marinade and mix thoroughly.

4 Arrange the vegetables on a nonstick baking tray and roast in the oven, turning occasionally, for 25–30 minutes, or until golden brown and tender. Add the tomatoes for the last 5 minutes of the cooking time, just to split the skins and warm slightly.

5 Mix the cream cheese, honey, and paprika together in a bowl.

6 Serve the vegetables with the cream cheese mixture, and sprinkled with chopped parsley.

zucchini & cheese gratin

ingredients

SERVES 4–6

2 oz/55 g unsalted butter

6 zucchini, sliced

salt and pepper

2 tbsp chopped fresh
tarragon or a mixture of
mint, tarragon, and
flat-leaf parsley

7 oz/200 g/2 cups Gruyère or
Parmesan cheese, grated

4fl oz/125 ml/$^1/_2$ cup milk

4fl oz/125 ml/$^1/_2$ cup heavy
cream

2 eggs

freshly grated nutmeg

method

1 Melt the butter in a large sauté pan or skillet over medium-high heat. Add the zucchini and sauté for 4–6 minutes, turning the slices over occasionally, until colored on both sides. Remove from the pan and drain on paper towels, then season with salt and pepper.

2 Spread half the zucchini over the bottom of a greased ovenproof serving dish. Sprinkle with half the herbs and 2 oz/55 g/$^3/_4$ cup of the cheese. Repeat these layers once more.

3 Mix the milk, cream, and eggs together and add nutmeg, salt, and pepper. Pour this liquid over the zucchini, then sprinkle the top with the remaining cheese.

4 Bake the gratin in a preheated oven, 350°F/ 180°C, for 35–45 minutes, or until it is set in the center and golden brown. Remove from the oven and let stand for 5 minutes before serving straight from the dish.

cherry tomato clafoutis

ingredients

SERVES 4–6

14 oz/400 g cherry tomatoes

3 tbsp chopped fresh flat-leaf parsley, snipped fresh chives, or finely shredded fresh basil

3$1/2$ oz/100 g/1 cup grated Gruyère cheese

2 oz/55 g/generous $1/3$ cup all-purpose flour

4 large eggs, lightly beaten

3 tbsp sour cream

8 fl oz/225 ml/1 cup milk

salt and pepper

method

1 Lightly grease an oval ovenproof dish. Arrange the cherry tomatoes in the dish and sprinkle with the herbs and half the cheese.

2 Put the flour in a mixing bowl, then slowly add the eggs, whisking until smooth. Whisk in the sour cream, then slowly whisk in the milk to make a thin, smooth batter. Season with salt and pepper.

3 Gently pour the batter over the tomatoes, then sprinkle the top with the remaining cheese. Bake in a preheated oven, 375°F/ 190°C, for 40–45 minutes, or until set and puffy, covering the top with foil if it browns too much before the batter sets. If serving hot, let the clafoutis cool for a few minutes before cutting, or let cool to room temperature.

caramelized onion tart

ingredients

SERVES 4–6

7 tbsp unsalted butter

1 lb 5 oz/600 g onions, thinly sliced

2 eggs

3¹/₂ fl oz/100 ml/generous ¹/₃ cup heavy cream

salt and pepper

3¹/₂ oz/100 g/generous ³/₄ cup grated Gruyère cheese

8-inch/20-cm ready-baked pastry shell

3¹/₂ oz/100 g/generous ³/₄ cup coarsely grated Parmesan cheese

method

1 Melt the butter in a heavy-bottom skillet over medium heat. Add the onions and cook, stirring frequently to avoid burning, for 30 minutes, or until well-browned and caramelized. Remove the onions from the skillet and set aside.

2 Beat the eggs in a large bowl, stir in the cream, and season with salt and pepper. Add the Gruyère and mix well. Stir in the cooked onions.

3 Pour the egg and onion mixture into the baked tart shell and sprinkle with the Parmesan cheese. Put on a cookie sheet. Bake in a preheated oven, 375°F/190°C, for 15–20 minutes until the filling has set and begun to brown.

4 Remove from the oven and let rest for at least 10 minutes. The tart can be served hot or left to cool to room temperature.

broccoli & sesame frittata

ingredients

SERVES 2

6 oz/175 g broccoli, broken
   into small florets
3 oz/85 g asparagus spears,
   sliced diagonally
1 tbsp virgin olive oil
1 onion, cut into small wedges
2–4 garlic cloves, finely
   chopped
1 large orange bell pepper,
   seeded and chopped
4 eggs
3 tbsp cold water
salt and pepper
1 oz/25 g/$\frac{1}{8}$ cup
   sesame seeds
$\frac{1}{2}$ oz/15 g/$\frac{1}{8}$ cup freshly
   grated Parmesan cheese
3 scallions, finely sliced

method

1 Cook the broccoli in a pan of lightly salted boiling water for 4 minutes. Add the asparagus after 2 minutes. Drain, then plunge into cold water. Drain again and set aside.

2 Heat the oil in a large skillet over low heat, add the onion, garlic, and orange bell pepper and cook, stirring frequently, for 8 minutes, or until the vegetables have softened.

3 Beat the eggs with the water, salt, and pepper in a medium-size bowl. Pour into the skillet, add the broccoli and asparagus, and stir gently. Cook over medium heat for 3–4 minutes, drawing the mixture from the edges of the skillet into the center, allowing the uncooked egg to flow to the edges of the skillet. Preheat the broiler.

4 Sprinkle the top of the frittata with the sesame seeds and cheese and cook under the preheated broiler for 3–5 minutes, or until golden and set. Sprinkle with the scallions, cut into wedges, and serve. Serve warm or cold.

baked eggs with cream, spinach & parmesan

ingredients

SERVES 2

2 tbsp butter, plus extra
   for greasing
$4^1/_2$ oz/125 g baby spinach
$^1/_2$ tsp freshly grated nutmeg
4 small eggs
2 fl oz/50 ml/$^1/_4$ cup
   light cream
2 tbsp freshly grated
   Parmesan cheese
salt and pepper

method

1 Lightly grease 2 individual ceramic gratin dishes, or similar.

2 Melt the butter in a large skillet over low heat and add the spinach. Cook for 1 minute, stirring with a wooden spoon until the spinach starts to wilt. Season with a little nutmeg, then divide among the prepared dishes.

3 Gently break 2 eggs into each dish. Pour the cream over them, and sprinkle with grated Parmesan, then season with salt and pepper. Bake in a preheated oven, 325°F/160°C, for 10 minutes, or until the whites of the eggs have set but the yolks remain runny. Serve at once.

mushroom stroganoff

ingredients

SERVES 4

1 lb 4 oz/550 g mixed fresh
   mushrooms, such as
   cremini, chanterelles,
   cèpes, and oyster
1 red onion, diced
2 garlic cloves, crushed
15 fl oz/425 ml/scant 2 cups
   vegetable stock
1 tbsp tomato paste
2 tbsp lemon juice
scant 1 tbsp cornstarch
2 tbsp cold water
4 oz/115 g/$^1/_2$ cup lowfat
   plain yogurt
3 tbsp chopped fresh parsley
pepper
boiled brown or white rice
   and crisp green salad,
   to serve

method

1 Put the mushrooms, onion, garlic, stock, tomato paste, and lemon juice into a pan and bring to a boil. Reduce the heat, cover, and let simmer for 15 minutes, or until the onion is tender.

2 Blend the cornstarch with the water in a small bowl and stir into the mushroom mixture. Return to a boil, stirring constantly, and cook until the sauce thickens. Reduce the heat and let simmer for an additional 2–3 minutes, stirring occasionally.

3 Just before serving, remove the pan from the heat, and stir in the yogurt, making sure that the stroganoff is not boiling or it may separate and curdle. Stir in 2 tablespoons of the parsley and season with pepper. Transfer the stroganoff to a warmed serving dish, sprinkle over the remaining parsley, and serve at once with boiled brown or white rice and a crisp green salad.

vegetable & coconut curry

ingredients

SERVES 4

1 onion, coarsely chopped

3 garlic cloves, thinly sliced

1-inch/2.5-cm piece fresh
    gingerroot, thinly sliced

2 fresh green chiles, seeded
    and finely chopped

1 tbsp vegetable oil

1 tsp ground turmeric

1 tsp ground coriander

1 tsp ground cumin

2 lb 4 oz/1 kg mixed
    vegetables, such as
    cauliflower, zucchini,
    potatoes, carrots, and
    green beans, cut into
    chunks

7 oz/200 g/scant 1 cup
    coconut cream
    or milk

salt and pepper

2 tbsp chopped fresh cilantro,
    to garnish

freshly cooked rice, to serve

method

1 Put the onion, garlic, gingerroot, and chiles in a food processor and process until almost smooth.

2 Heat the oil in a large, heavy-bottom pan over medium-low heat, add the onion mixture, and cook, stirring constantly, for 5 minutes.

3 Add the turmeric, coriander, and cumin and cook, stirring frequently, for 3–4 minutes. Add the vegetables and stir well to coat in the spice paste.

4 Add the coconut cream or milk to the vegetables, cover, and let simmer for 30–40 minutes until the vegetables are tender.

5 Season with salt and pepper, garnish with the chopped fresh cilantro, and serve with rice.

Thai yellow vegetable curry with brown basmati rice

ingredients

SERVES 4

$1^3/4$ oz/50 g yellow bell
    pepper, seeded
$1^3/4$ oz/50 g celery
$1^3/4$ oz/50 g baby corn
3 oz/85 g leek
$3^1/2$ oz/100 g sweet potato
$3^1/2$ oz/100 g bok choy
$1^3/4$ oz/50 g zucchini
$1^3/4$ oz/50 g snow peas
10 fl oz/300 ml/$1^1/4$ cups
    pineapple juice
7 fl oz/200 ml/scant 1 cup
    water
3 tbsp lime juice
2 tbsp cornstarch
4 tbsp lowfat plain yogurt
4 tbsp chopped fresh cilantro
$5^1/2$ oz/150 g cooked brown
    basmati rice

spice mix

1 tsp finely chopped garlic
$1/4$ tsp ground turmeric
1 tsp ground coriander
1 tsp finely chopped
    lemongrass
3 kaffir lime leaves
1 tsp finely chopped green
    chile

method

1 To make the spice mix, pound all the spices to a fine paste using a mortar and pestle.

2 To prepare the vegetables, cut the yellow bell pepper into $1/2$-inch/1-cm squares, cut the celery, baby corn, and leek into $1/4$-inch/ 5-mm lengths, and cut the sweet potato into $1/2$-inch/1-cm cubes. Shred the bok choy. Cut the zucchini into $1/4$-inch/5-mm cubes and slice the snow peas into thin strips.

3 Put the pepper, celery, baby corn, leek, sweet potato, pineapple juice, water, and the spice mix into a large pan with a lid and bring to a boil. Reduce the heat and skim the scum from the surface with a metal spoon. Cover and let simmer for 15 minutes.

4 Add the bok choy, zucchini, and snow peas and cook for 2 minutes. Add the lime juice, then gradually add the cornstarch blended with a little cold water. Cook, stirring constantly, until thickened to the required consistency.

5 Remove the curry from the heat and let cool for 2–3 minutes. Stir in the yogurt. (Do not boil once the yogurt has been added or the curry will separate.) Stir in the fresh cilantro and serve the curry with the rice.

roasted garlic mashed potatoes

ingredients

SERVES 4

2 whole garlic bulbs

1 tbsp olive oil

2 lb/900 g mealy potatoes, peeled

4 fl oz/125 ml/$^1/_2$ cup milk

2 oz/55 g butter

salt and pepper

method

1 Separate the garlic cloves, place on a large piece of foil, and drizzle with the oil. Wrap the garlic in the foil and roast in a preheated oven, 350°F/180°C, for about 1 hour, or until very tender. Let cool slightly.

2 Meanwhile, cut the potatoes into chunks, then cook in a pan of lightly salted boiling water for 15 minutes, or until tender.

3 Squeeze the cooled garlic cloves out of their skins and push through a strainer into a pan. Add the milk and butter and season with salt and pepper. Heat gently until the butter has melted.

4 Drain the cooked potatoes, then mash in the pan until smooth. Pour in the garlic mixture and heat gently, stirring, until the ingredients are combined. Serve hot.

roasted squash wedges

ingredients

SERVES 4

7 oz/200 g acorn squash
   or other type of squash,
   peeled, seeded, and cut
   into 4 wedges
1 tsp vegetable oil
$3^1/_2$ oz/100 g onion,
   finely chopped
1 tsp minced garlic
$2^1/_2$ oz/70 g three-grain risotto
   mix (baldo rice, spelt, and
   pearl barley—this is
   available ready-mixed)
10 fl oz/300 ml/$1^1/_4$ cups
   vegetable stock
8 oz/225 g asparagus tips
2 tbsp finely chopped fresh
   marjoram, plus extra
   to garnish
3 tbsp lowfat cream cheese
2 tbsp finely chopped
   fresh parsley
pepper

method

1 Spread out the squash wedges on a nonstick cookie sheet and roast in a preheated oven, 400°F/200°C, for 20 minutes, or until tender and golden brown.

2 Meanwhile, heat the oil in a medium pan over high heat, add the onion and garlic, and cook, stirring, until softened but not colored. Add the risotto mix and stir in half the stock. Let simmer, stirring occasionally, until the stock has reduced in the pan. Pour in the remaining stock and continue to cook, stirring occasionally, until the grains are tender.

3 Cut 6 oz/175g of the asparagus into 4-inch/ 10-cm lengths and blanch in a pan of boiling water for 2 minutes. Drain and keep warm. Cut the remaining asparagus into 1/4-inch/ 5-mm slices and add to the risotto for the last 3 minutes of the cooking time.

4 Remove the risotto from the heat and stir in the marjoram, cream cheese, and parsley. Season with pepper. Do not reboil.

5 To serve, lay the squash wedges on warmed serving plates, then spoon over the risotto and top with the asparagus. Garnish with marjoram.

stir-fried broccoli

ingredients

SERVES 4

2 tbsp vegetable oil

2 broccoli heads,
    cut into florets

2 tbsp soy sauce

1 tsp cornstarch

1 tbsp superfine sugar

1 tsp grated fresh gingerroot

1 garlic clove, crushed

pinch of dried red pepper flakes

1 tsp toasted sesame seeds,
    to garnish

method

1 Heat the oil in a large preheated wok or skillet over high heat until almost smoking. Add the broccoli and stir-fry for 4–5 minutes. Reduce the heat to medium.

2 Combine the soy sauce, cornstarch, sugar, gingerroot, garlic, and red pepper flakes in a small bowl. Add the mixture to the broccoli and cook, stirring constantly, for 2–3 minutes until the sauce thickens slightly.

3 Transfer to a warmed serving dish, garnish with the sesame seeds, and serve immediately.

roasted onions

ingredients

SERVES 4

8 large onions, peeled

3 tbsp olive oil

2 oz/55 g butter

2 tsp chopped fresh thyme

salt and pepper

7 oz/200 g/1 cup Cheddar
    cheese, grated

method

1 Cut a cross down through the top of the onions towards the root, without cutting all the way through. Place the onions in a roasting pan and drizzle over the olive oil.

2 Press a little of the butter into the open crosses, sprinkle with the thyme, and season with salt and pepper. Cover with foil and roast in a preheated oven, 350°F/180°C, for 40–45 minutes.

3 Remove from the oven, take off the foil and baste the onions with the pan juices. Return to the oven and cook for a further 15 minutes, uncovered, to allow the onions to brown.

4 Take the onions out of the oven and scatter the grated cheese over them. Return them to the oven for a few minutes so that the cheese starts to melt. Serve immediately.

brussels sprouts with chestnuts

ingredients

SERVES 4

1 lb/450 g Brussels sprouts

4 oz/115 g/¹/₂ cup unsalted butter

2 oz/55 g/generous ¹/₄ cup brown sugar

4 oz/115 g cooked and peeled chestnuts

method

1 Trim the Brussels sprouts and remove and discard any loose outer leaves. Add to a large pan of boiling salted water and boil for 5–10 minutes until just tender, but not too soft. Drain well, refresh under cold water, and drain again. Set aside.

2 Melt the butter in a heavy-bottom skillet over medium heat. Add the sugar and stir until dissolved. Add the chestnuts and cook, stirring occasionally, until well coated and beginning to brown.

3 Add the sprouts to the chestnuts and mix well. Reduce the heat and cook gently, stirring occasionally, for 3–4 minutes to heat through.

4 Remove from the heat, transfer to a warmed serving dish, and serve immediately.

tabbouleh

ingredients

SERVES 4

6 oz/175 g/scant 1 cup
  bulgur wheat
3 tbsp extra-virgin olive oil
4 tbsp lemon juice
salt and pepper
4 scallions
1 green bell pepper,
  seeded and sliced
4 tomatoes, chopped
2 tbsp chopped fresh parsley
2 tbsp chopped fresh mint
8 black olives, pitted

method

1 Place the bulgur wheat in a large bowl and add enough cold water to cover. Let stand for 30 minutes, or until the wheat has doubled in size. Drain well and press out as much liquid as possible. Spread out the wheat on paper towels to dry.

2 Place the wheat in a serving bowl. Mix the olive oil and lemon juice together in a pitcher and season with salt and pepper. Pour the lemon mixture over the wheat and let marinate for 1 hour.

3 Using a sharp knife, finely chop the scallions, then add to the salad with the green bell pepper, tomatoes, parsley, and mint and toss lightly to mix. Top the salad with the olives and serve immediately.

papaya, avocado & red bell pepper salad

ingredients

SERVES 4–6

7 oz/200 g mixed salad greens

2–3 scallions, chopped

3–4 tbsp chopped fresh cilantro

1 small papaya

2 red bell peppers

1 avocado

1 tbsp lime juice

3–4 tbsp pumpkin seeds,
    preferably toasted (optional)

dressing

juice of 1 lime

large pinch of paprika

large pinch of ground cumin

large pinch of sugar

1 garlic clove, finely chopped

4 tbsp extra-virgin olive oil

salt

dash of white wine vinegar
    (optional)

method

1 Combine the salad greens with the scallions and cilantro in a bowl. Mix well, then transfer the salad to a large serving dish.

2 Cut the papaya in half and scoop out the seeds with a spoon. Cut into fourths, remove the peel, and slice the flesh. Arrange on top of the salad greens. Cut the bell peppers in half, remove the cores and seeds, then thinly slice. Add the bell peppers to the salad greens.

3 Cut the avocado in half around the pit. Twist apart, then remove the pit with a knife. Carefully peel off the skin, dice the flesh, and toss in lime juice to prevent discoloration. Add to the other salad ingredients.

4 To make the dressing, whisk the lime juice, paprika, cumin, sugar, garlic, and oil together in a small bowl. Season with salt.

5 Pour the dressing over the salad and toss lightly, adding a dash of wine vinegar if a flavor with more 'bite' is preferred. Sprinkle with pumpkin seeds, if using.

avocado salad with lime dressing

ingredients

SERVES 4

2^1/$_4$ oz/60 g mixed red and
   green lettuce leaves

2^1/$_4$ oz/60 g wild arugula

4 scallions, finely diced

5 tomatoes, sliced

1 oz/25 g/^{1}/$_4$ cup walnuts,
   toasted and chopped

2 avocados

1 tbsp lemon juice

lime dressing

1 tbsp lime juice

1 tsp French mustard

1 tbsp sour cream

1 tbsp chopped fresh parsley
   or cilantro

3 tbsp extra-virgin olive oil

pinch of sugar

salt and pepper

method

1 Wash and drain the lettuce and arugula, if necessary. Shred all the leaves and arrange in the bottom of a large salad bowl. Add the scallions, tomatoes, and walnuts.

2 Pit, peel, and thinly slice or dice the avocados. Brush with the lemon juice to prevent discoloration, then transfer to the salad bowl. Gently mix together.

3 To make the dressing, put all the dressing ingredients in a screw-top jar and shake well. Drizzle over the salad and serve immediately.

roasted bell pepper salad

ingredients

SERVES 8

3 red bell peppers

3 yellow bell peppers

5 tbsp Spanish extra-virgin
    olive oil

2 tbsp dry sherry vinegar or
    lemon juice

2 garlic cloves, crushed

pinch of sugar

salt and pepper

1 tbsp capers

8 small black Spanish olives

2 tbsp chopped fresh
    marjoram, plus extra
    sprigs to garnish

method

1 Preheat the broiler to high. Place the bell peppers on a wire rack or broiler pan and cook under the broiler for 10 minutes, until their skins have blackened and blistered, turning them frequently.

2 Remove the roasted bell peppers from the heat, and either put them in a bowl and immediately cover tightly with a clean, damp dish towel, or put them in a plastic bag. The steam helps to soften the skins and makes it easier to remove them. Let stand for about 15 minutes, until cool enough to handle.

3 Holding one bell pepper at a time over a clean bowl, use a sharp knife to make a small hole in the base and gently squeeze out the juices and reserve them. Still holding the bell pepper over the bowl, carefully peel off the blackened skin with your fingers, or a knife, and discard it. Cut the bell peppers in half and remove the stem, core, and seeds, then cut each bell pepper into neat thin strips. Arrange the bell pepper strips on a serving dish.

4 To the reserved pepper juices add the olive oil, sherry vinegar, garlic, sugar, salt, and pepper. Whisk together until combined. Drizzle the dressing evenly over the salad.

5 Sprinkle the capers, olives, and chopped marjoram over the salad, garnish with marjoram sprigs, and serve at room temperature.

green bean salad with feta cheese

ingredients

SERVES 4

12 oz/350 g green beans

1 red onion, chopped

3–4 tbsp chopped fresh
 cilantro

2 radishes, thinly sliced

2³/4 oz/75 g feta cheese
 drained weight, crumbled

1 tsp chopped fresh oregano,
 plus extra leaves to garnish
 (optional), or ¹/2 tsp dried

pepper

2 tbsp red wine or fruit vinegar

3 fl oz/80 ml/¹/3 cup extra-
 virgin olive oil

3 ripe tomatoes, cut into
 wedges

slices of crusty bread,
 to serve

method

1 Bring about 2 inches/5 cm of water to a boil in the bottom of a steamer. Add the beans to the top part of the steamer, cover, and steam for 5 minutes, or until just tender.

2 Place the beans in a large bowl and add the onion, cilantro, radishes, and feta cheese.

3 Sprinkle the oregano over the salad, then season with pepper. Mix the vinegar and oil together in a small bowl and pour over the salad. Toss gently to mix well.

4 Transfer to a serving platter, surround with the tomato wedges, and serve at once with slices of crusty bread, or cover and chill until ready to serve.

greek salad

ingredients

SERVES 4

4 tomatoes, cut into wedges

1 onion, sliced

^{1}/$_2$ cucumber, sliced

8 oz/225 g/1^1/$_2$ cups
   kalamata olives, stoned

8 oz/225 g feta cheese,
   cubed

2 tbsp fresh cilantro leaves

fresh flat-leaf parsley sprigs,
   to garnish

pita bread, to serve

dressing

5 tbsp extra-virgin olive oil

2 tbsp white wine vinegar

1 tbsp lemon juice

^{1}/$_2$ tsp sugar

1 tbsp chopped fresh cilantro

salt and pepper

method

1 To make the dressing, put all the ingredients for the dressing into a large bowl and mix well together.

2 Add the tomatoes, onion, cucumber, olives, cheese, and cilantro. Toss all the ingredients together, then divide among individual serving bowls. Garnish with parsley sprigs and serve with pita bread.

desserts

Vegetarians usually take a great interest in the nutritional content of their food and have often chosen this lifestyle with a view to becoming healthier and remaining that way. This does not mean, however, that vegetarians do not enjoy an occasional dessert!

This chapter has a mix of dessert recipes, some of which are health-conscious and some of which are completely indulgent for those days when nothing less will do. If you follow a lowfat diet, choose the Icy Fruit Blizzard, Apricot & Passion Fruit Sorbet, or the Blueberry Frozen Yogurt, which is also a treat for diabetics. The Baked Apricots with Honey, Blueberry Filo Tart, and Spiced Baked Goat Yogurt are also lowfat.

If you want to relax just a little, try the Raspberry Ripple Ice Cream, Lemon Yogurt Ice Cream, Creamy Mango Brûlée, Mascarpone Creams, Creamy Chocolate Dessert, or the Summer Dessert.

And if you want to go completely wild? Well, three obvious choices are the Banana Toffee Pies, the Mississippi Mud Pie, and the Chocolate Fudge Tart. Spanish Caramel Custard will also fit the bill, and if you want to be really naughty, make the Rich Vanilla Ice Cream and serve it with homemade Apple Pie—two in one!

raspberry ripple ice cream

ingredients

SERVES 6

3 oz/85 g/^{3}/$_8$ cup fresh or
frozen raspberries,
thawed if frozen, plus
extra to serve

2 tbsp water

2 eggs

1 tbsp superfine sugar

10 fl oz/300 ml/1^1/$_4$ cups
milk, warmed

1 tsp vanilla extract

10 fl oz/300 ml/1^1/$_4$ cups
heavy cream

method

1 Turn the freezer to rapid. Put the raspberries into a pan with the water and bring to a boil, then reduce the heat and let simmer gently for 5 minutes. Remove from the heat and let cool for 30 minutes. Transfer to a food processor or blender and process to a purée, then rub through a nylon strainer to remove the pips. Set aside.

2 Beat the eggs in a bowl. Stir the sugar into the warmed milk, then slowly pour onto the eggs, beating constantly. Strain into a clean pan and cook over low heat, stirring constantly, for 8–10 minutes, or until the custard thickens and coats the back of a wooden spoon. Add the vanilla extract, remove from the heat, and let cool.

3 Half-whip the cream in a large bowl, then slowly stir in the cooled custard. Pour into a freezerproof container and freeze for 1^1/2 hours, or until starting to set around the outside. Remove from the freezer and stir the mixture, breaking up any ice crystals.

4 Return the mixture to the freezer and freeze for an additional hour, then remove from the freezer again and gently stir in the raspberry purée to give a rippled effect. Return to the freezer for an additional hour or until frozen. Serve in scoops with extra fresh raspberries.

rich vanilla ice cream

ingredients

SERVES 4–6

10 fl oz/300 ml/1^1/$_4$ cups light cream and 10 fl oz/300 ml/1^1/$_4$ cups heavy cream or 20 fl oz/625 ml/2^1/$_2$ cups heavy whipping cream

1 vanilla bean

4 large egg yolks

3^1/$_2$ oz/100 g/generous ^{1}/$_2$ cup superfine sugar

method

1 Pour the light and heavy cream or heavy whipping cream into a large heavy-bottom pan. Split open the vanilla bean and scrape out the seeds into the cream, then add the whole vanilla bean too. Bring almost to a boil, then remove from the heat and let infuse for 30 minutes.

2 Put the egg yolks and sugar in a large bowl and whisk together until pale and the mixture leaves a trail when the whisk is lifted. Remove the vanilla bean from the cream, then slowly add the cream to the egg mixture, stirring all the time with a wooden spoon. Strain the mixture into the rinsed-out pan or a double boiler and cook over low heat for 10–15 minutes, stirring all the time, until the mixture thickens enough to coat the back of the spoon. Do not let the mixture boil or it will curdle. Remove the custard from the heat and let cool for at least 1 hour, stirring from time to time to prevent a skin forming.

3 Churn the custard in an ice-cream maker following the manufacturer's instructions. Serve immediately if wished, or transfer to a freezerproof container, cover with a lid, and store in the freezer.

lemon yogurt ice cream

ingredients

SERVES 4–6

2–3 lemons

20 fl oz/625 ml/scant $2^{1}/_{2}$ cups strained plain yogurt

5 fl oz/150 ml/$^{2}/_{3}$ cup heavy cream

$3^{1}/_{2}$ oz/100 g/$^{1}/_{2}$ cup superfine sugar

finely pared orange zest, to garnish

method

1 Squeeze the juice from the lemons—you need 6 tablespoons in total. Put the juice into a bowl, add the yogurt, cream, and sugar, and mix well together.

2 If using an ice-cream machine, churn the mixture in the machine following the manufacturer's instructions. Alternatively, freeze the mixture in a freezerproof container, uncovered, for 1–2 hours, or until it starts to set around the edges. Turn the mixture into a bowl and stir with a fork or beat in a food processor until smooth. Return to the freezer and freeze for an additional 2–3 hours, or until firm or required. Cover the container with a lid for storing. Serve with finely pared orange zest.

icy fruit blizzard

ingredients

SERVES 4

1 pineapple

1 large piece seeded
   watermelon, peeled and
   cut into small pieces

8 oz/225 g/1^{1}/$_{2}$ cups
   strawberries or other
   berries, hulled and left
   whole or sliced

1 mango, peach, or nectarine,
   peeled and sliced

1 banana, peeled and sliced

orange juice

superfine sugar, to taste

method

1 Cover 2 nonstick cookie sheets or ordinary cookie sheets with a sheet of plastic wrap. Arrange the fruits on top and open freeze for at least 2 hours, or until firm and icy.

2 Place one type of fruit in a food processor and process until it is all broken up into small pieces.

3 Add a little orange juice and sugar to taste, and continue to process until it forms a granular mixture. Repeat with the remaining fruits. Arrange in chilled bowls and serve immediately.

blueberry frozen yogurt

ingredients

SERVES 4

6 oz/175g/³/₄ cup fresh
    blueberries
finely grated rind and
    juice of 1 orange
3 tbsp maple syrup
1 lb 2 oz/500 g plain
    lowfat yogurt

method

1 Put the blueberries and orange juice into a food processor or blender and process to a purée. Strain through a nylon strainer into a bowl or pitcher.

2 Stir the maple syrup and yogurt together in a large mixing bowl, then fold in the fruit purée.

3 Churn the mixture in an ice-cream machine, following the manufacturer's instructions, then freeze for 5–6 hours. If you don't have an ice-cream machine, transfer the mixture to a freezerproof container, and freeze for 2 hours. Remove from the freezer, turn out into a bowl, and beat until smooth. Return to the freezer and freeze until firm.

apricot & passion fruit sorbet

ingredients

sorbet

$3^1/_2$ oz/100 g no-soak dried
   apricots
9 fl oz/250 ml/generous
   1 cup water
2 tbsp freshly squeezed
   lemon juice
2 tbsp freshly squeezed
   orange juice
7 tbsp passion fruit pulp,
   strained to remove
   the seeds

sesame snaps

1 tbsp sesame seeds
1 tbsp liquid glucose
3 tbsp superfine sugar
2 tbsp all-purpose flour

method

1 To make the sorbet, put the apricots in a pan with the water and bring to a boil. Reduce the heat and let simmer for 10–15 minutes, or until soft. Remove from the heat. Purée the apricots in a food processor with the water, then blend in the lemon juice, orange juice, and 3 tbsp of the passion fruit pulp.

2 Add 2 tbsp of the passion fruit pulp, mix well, then transfer to a large, freezerproof container and freeze for 20 minutes. Beat the sorbet to break down the ice crystals, then return to the freezer. Freeze for an additional 2 hours, or until fully frozen, beating every 20 minutes to give a smooth texture to the finished sorbet.

3 To make the sesame snaps, toss the sesame seeds in a small pan over high heat until golden brown. Remove from the heat, add the glucose, sugar, and flour and mix with a metal spoon to form a sticky paste. Remove from the pan and let cool slightly. Roll the paste into a sausage shape and cut into 16 pieces. With wet hands, roll each piece into a small ball, then lightly press out on to a sheet of silicone.

4 Bake in a preheated oven, 350°F/180°C, for 6 minutes until golden brown. Transfer to a wire rack and let cool. Serve the sorbet with the remaining passion fruit pulp spooned over and the sesame snaps to accompany.

spanish caramel custard

ingredients

SERVES 6

18 fl oz/500 ml/scant
   2¹/₂ cups whole milk
¹/₂ orange with 2 long, thin
   pieces of rind pared off
   and reserved
1 vanilla bean, split, or
   ¹/₂ tsp vanilla extract
6 oz/175 g/scant 1 cup
   superfine sugar
butter, for greasing the dish
3 large eggs, plus 2 large
   egg yolks

method

1 Pour the milk into a pan with the orange zest and vanilla bean or extract. Bring to a boil, then remove from the heat and stir in 3 oz/85g/¹/₂ cup of the sugar; set aside for at least 30 minutes to infuse.

2 Meanwhile, put the remaining sugar and 4 tablespoons of water in another pan over medium-high heat. Stir until the sugar dissolves, then boil without stirring until the caramel turns deep golden brown. Immediately remove the pan from the heat and squeeze in a few drops of orange juice to stop the cooking. Pour into a lightly buttered 32-fl oz/1-liter/5-cup soufflé dish and swirl to cover the base; set aside.

3 Return the pan of infused milk to the heat, and bring to a simmer. Beat the whole eggs and egg yolks together in a heatproof bowl. Pour the warm milk into the eggs, whisking constantly. Strain into the soufflé dish.

4 Place the soufflé dish in a roasting pan and pour in enough boiling water to come halfway up the sides of the dish. Bake in a preheated oven, 325°F/160°C, for 75–90 minutes until set and a knife inserted in the center comes out clean. Remove the soufflé dish from the roasting pan and set aside to cool completely. Cover and let chill overnight. To serve, run a metal spatula round the soufflé, then invert onto a serving plate, shaking firmly to release.

creamy mango brûlée

ingredients

SERVES 4

2 mangoes

9 oz/250 g/generous 1 cup
    mascarpone cheese

7 fl oz/200 ml/generous
    3/4 cup strained plain
    yogurt

1 tsp ground ginger

grated rind and juice of 1 lime

2 tbsp soft light brown sugar

8 tbsp raw brown sugar

method

1 Slice the mangoes on either side of the pit. Discard the pit and peel the fruit. Slice and then chop the fruit. Divide it among 4 ramekins.

2 Beat the mascarpone cheese with the yogurt. Fold in the ginger, lime rind and juice, and soft brown sugar. Divide the mixture among the ramekins and level off the tops. Chill for 2 hours.

3 Sprinkle 2 tablespoons of raw brown sugar over the top of each dish, covering the creamy mixture. Place under a hot broiler for 2–3 minutes, until melted and browned. Let cool, then chill until needed. This dessert should be eaten on the day it is made.

mascarpone creams

ingredients

SERVES 4

4 oz/115 g Amaretti cookies,
    crushed

4 tbsp Amaretto or
    Maraschino

4 eggs, separated

2 oz/55 g/generous 1/4 cup
    superfine sugar

8 oz/225 g/1 cup Mascarpone
    cheese

toasted slivered almonds,
    to decorate

method

1 Place the Amaretti crumbs in a bowl, add the Amaretto or Maraschino, and set aside to soak.

2 Meanwhile, beat the egg yolks with the superfine sugar until pale and thick. Fold in the Mascarpone and soaked cookie crumbs.

3 Whisk the egg whites in a separate, spotlessly clean bowl until stiff, then gently fold into the cheese mixture. Divide the Mascarpone cream among 4 serving dishes and let chill for 1–2 hours. Sprinkle with toasted slivered almonds just before serving.

creamy chocolate dessert

ingredients

SERVES 4-6

6 oz/175 g semisweet
   chocolate, at least
   70% cocoa solids,
   broken up
$1^1/_2$ tbsp orange juice
3 tbsp water
2 tbsp unsalted butter, diced
2 eggs, separated
$^1/_8$ tsp cream of tartar
3 tbsp superfine sugar
6 tbsp heavy cream

pistachio-orange praline

corn oil, for greasing
2 oz/55 g/generous $^1/_4$ cup
   superfine sugar
2 oz/55 g/scant $^1/_2$ cup
   shelled pistachios
finely grated rind of
   1 large orange

method

1 Melt the chocolate with the orange juice and water in a small pan over very low heat, stirring constantly. Remove from the heat and melt in the butter until incorporated. Using a rubber spatula, scrape the chocolate into a bowl. Beat the egg yolks until blended, then beat them into the chocolate mixture. Set aside to cool.

2 In a clean bowl, whisk the egg whites with the cream of tartar until soft peaks form. Gradually beat in the sugar, 1 tablespoon at a time, beating well after each addition, until the meringue is glossy. Beat 1 tablespoon of the meringue mixture into the chocolate mixture, then fold in the rest.

3 In a separate bowl, whip the cream until soft peaks form. Fold into the chocolate mixture. Spoon into individual glass bowls or wine glasses, or 1 large serving bowl. Cover with plastic wrap and let chill for at least 4 hours.

4 To make the praline, lightly grease a cookie sheet with corn oil and set aside. Put the sugar and pistachios in a small pan over medium heat. When the sugar starts to melt, stir gently until a liquid caramel forms and the nuts start popping. Pour the praline onto the cookie sheet and immediately finely grate the orange rind over. Let cool until firm then coarsely chop. Just before serving, sprinkle the praline over the chocolate pudding.

summer dessert

ingredients

SERVES 6

1 lb 8 oz/675 g mixed soft
   fruits, such as red
   currants, black currants,
   raspberries, and
   blackberries
5 oz/140 g superfine sugar
2 tbsp crème de framboise
   liqueur (optional)
6–8 slices of good day-old
   white bread, crusts removed
heavy cream, to serve

method

1 Place the fruits in a large pan with the sugar. Over low heat, very slowly bring to a boil, stirring carefully to ensure that the sugar has dissolved. Cook over low heat for only 2–3 minutes, until the juices run but the fruit still holds its shape. Add the liqueur if using.

2 Line a 28-fl oz/875-ml/3^{1}/$_{2}$-cup pudding bowl with some of the slices of bread (cut them to shape so that the bread fits well). Spoon in the cooked fruit and juices, reserving a little of the juice for later.

3 Cover the surface of the fruit with the remaining bread. Place a plate on top of the pudding and weight it down for at least 8 hours or overnight in the refrigerator.

4 Turn out the pudding and pour over the reserved juices to color any white bits of bread that may still be showing. Serve with the heavy cream.

baked apricots with honey

ingredients

SERVES 4

butter, for greasing

4 apricots, each cut in half
    and pitted

4 tbsp slivered almonds

4 tbsp honey

pinch ground ginger or grated
    nutmeg

method

1 Lightly butter an ovenproof dish large enough to hold the apricot halves in a single layer.

2 Arrange the apricot halves in the dish, cut side up. Sprinkle with the almonds and drizzle the honey over. Dust with the spice.

3 Bake in a preheated oven, 400°F/200°C, for 12–15 minutes until the apricots are tender and the almonds golden. Remove from the oven and serve at once.

apple pie

ingredients

pie dough

7 oz/200 g/1^1/$_4$ cups all-
   purpose flour, plus extra
   for dusting
3^1/$_2$ oz/100 g butter, diced,
   plus extra for greasing
1^3/$_4$ oz/50 g/scant ^{1}/$_3$ cup
   confectioners' sugar, sifted
finely grated rind of 1 lemon
1 egg yolk, beaten
3 tbsp milk

filling

3 cooking apples
2 tbsp lemon juice
finely grated rind of 1 lemon
5 fl oz/150 ml/^{2}/$_3$ cup
   clear honey
6 oz/175 g/3 cups fresh
   white or whole wheat
   bread crumbs
1 tsp ground mixed spice
pinch of freshly grated nutmeg

whipped heavy cream,
   to serve

method

1 To make the pie dough, sift the flour into a mixing bowl, then rub in the butter. Mix in the sugar, lemon rind, egg yolk, and milk. Knead briefly on a lightly floured counter, then let rest for 30 minutes.

2 Roll out the pie dough to a thickness of ^{1}/4 inch/5 mm and use it to line the base and sides of a greased 8-inch/20-cm tart pan.

3 To make the filling, core 2 cooking apples and grate them into a bowl. Add 1 tablespoon of the lemon juice and all the lemon rind, along with the honey, bread crumbs, and mixed spice. Mix together well, then spoon evenly into the pie shell.

4 Core and slice the remaining apple, and use to decorate the top of the pie. Brush the apple slices with the remaining lemon juice, then sprinkle over the nutmeg. Bake the pie in a preheated oven, 400°F/200°C, for 35 minutes, or until it is firm. Remove from the oven and serve with whipped cream.

creamy rice dessert

ingredients

SERVES 4

1 tbsp butter, for greasing

3 oz/85 g/^{1}/$_2$ cup
golden raisins

5 tbsp superfine sugar

3^1/$_4$ oz/90 g/^{2}/$_3$ cup sweet rice

40 fl oz/1.25 liters/5 cups
milk

1 tsp vanilla extract

finely grated rind of 1 large
lemon

pinch of nutmeg

chopped pistachios,
to decorate

method

1 Grease a 32-fl oz/875-ml/3^1/$_2$-cup ovenproof dish with the butter.

2 Put the golden raisins, sugar, and rice into a mixing bowl, then stir in the milk and vanilla extract. Transfer to the greased ovenproof dish, sprinkle over the grated lemon rind and the nutmeg, then bake in a preheated oven, 325°F/160°C, for 2^1/$_2$ hours.

3 Remove from the oven and transfer to individual serving bowls. Decorate with chopped pistachios and serve.

banana toffee pies

ingredients

SERVES 4

two cans sweetened
   condensed milk, about
   14 fl oz/400 ml each
6 tbsp butter, melted
5^1/$_2$ oz/150 g graham crackers,
   crushed into crumbs
1^3/$_4$ oz/50 g/^{1}/$_3$ cup almonds,
   toasted and ground
1^3/$_4$ oz/50 g/^{1}/$_3$ cup
   hazelnuts, toasted
   and ground
4 ripe bananas
1 tbsp lemon juice
1 tsp vanilla extract
2^3/$_4$ oz/75 g chocolate flakes
16 fl oz/450 ml/scant 2 cups
   thick heavy cream,
   whipped

method

1 Place the cans of milk in a large pan and cover them with water. Bring to a boil, then reduce the heat and let simmer for 2 hours, topping up the water level regularly to keep the cans covered. Carefully lift out the hot cans and let cool.

2 Grease 4 individual loose-bottom tartlet pans with butter. Put the remaining butter into a bowl and add the crackers and nuts. Mix together well, then press the mixture evenly into the bottom of the tartlet pans. Bake in a preheated oven, 350°F/180°C, for 10–12 minutes, then remove from the oven and let cool.

3 Open the cans of condensed milk and spread the contents over the cracker layer in the tartlet pans. Peel and slice the bananas and put them into a bowl. Sprinkle over the lemon juice and vanilla extract and mix gently. Spoon the banana mixture on to the condensed milk layer, then top with a dollop of whipped cream. Break up the chocolate flakes, scatter over the tartlets, and serve.

blueberry filo tart

ingredients

SERVES 2

4 sheets of filo pastry

rapeseed or vegetable oil spray

7 oz/200 g/1 cup Mascarpone
    cheese

1 tsp honey

1 tbsp finely grated
    lemon rind

3 tbsp lemon juice

1 tsp superfine sugar

$3^{1}/_{2}$ oz/100 g fresh blueberries

method

1 Using a plate as a guide, cut out 4 x $5^{1}/_{2}$-inch/14-cm circles of filo pastry (you need two circles per tartlet). Spray each lightly with oil before laying two circles into 2 x 4-inch/10-cm fluted tartlet pans, pressing the pastry into the corners. Prick the bases with a fork.

2 Put a ramekin into the center of each tartlet shell to prevent the pastry rising, then bake in a preheated oven, 350°F/180°C, for 5 minutes. Remove the ramekins and bake the cases for an additional 4–5 minutes so that the bases cook. Remove from the oven and leave the shells to cool in the tins. Store in an airtight tin so that they remain crisp.

3 Mix the Mascarpone cheese with the honey in a small bowl.

4 Put the lemon rind and juice and the sugar in a small pan over low heat and heat until the liquid has evaporated, then add the blueberries. Stir with a metal spoon to coat the berries in the syrup. Remove from the heat and keep warm.

5 To serve, place each tartlet shell on a serving plate, add a spoonful of the Mascarpone mixture, then spoon over the warmed blueberries.

mississippi mud pie

ingredients

pie dough

9 oz/250 g/scant 1⁵/₈ cups
    all-purpose flour, plus
    extra for dusting
2 tbsp unsweetened cocoa
5 oz/140 g butter
2 tbsp superfine sugar
1–2 tbsp cold water

filling

6 oz/175 g butter
9 oz/250 g/scant 1³/₄ cups
    packed brown sugar
4 eggs, lightly beaten
4 tbsp unsweetened cocoa,
    sifted
5¹/₂ oz/150 g semisweet
    chocolate
10 fl oz/300 ml/1¹/₄ cups
    light cream
1 tsp chocolate extract
15 fl oz/425 ml/scant 2 cups
    whipped heavy cream and
    chocolate flakes and curls,
    to decorate

method

1 To make the pie dough, sift the flour and cocoa into a mixing bowl. Rub in the butter with your fingertips until the mixture resembles fine bread crumbs. Stir in the sugar and enough cold water to mix to a soft dough. Wrap the dough and let chill in the refrigerator for 15 minutes.

2 Roll out the dough on a lightly floured counter and use to line a 9-inch/23-cm loose-bottom tart pan or ceramic pie dish. Line with parchment paper and fill with dried beans. Bake in a preheated oven, 375°F/190°C, for 15 minutes. Remove from the oven and take out the paper and beans. Bake the pie shell for an additional 10 minutes.

3 To make the filling, beat the butter and sugar together in a bowl and gradually beat in the eggs, with the cocoa. Melt the chocolate and beat it into the mixture, with the light cream and the chocolate extract.

4 Reduce the oven temperature to 325°F/160°C. Pour the mixture into the pie shell and bake for 45 minutes, or until the filling has set gently. Let cool completely, then transfer to a serving plate.

5 Cover the mud pie with the whipped cream, decorate with chocolate flakes and curls and let chill until ready to serve.

chestnut, maple syrup & pecan tart

ingredients

SERVES 6

pie dough

4 oz/115 g/generous $^3/_4$ cup
 all-purpose flour

pinch of salt

2$^1/_2$ oz/75 g cold butter,
 cut into pieces

cold water

filling

2 lb 4 oz/1 kg canned
 sweetened chestnut purée

10 fl oz/300 ml/1$^1/_4$ cups
 heavy cream

2 tbsp butter

2 tbsp maple syrup

6 oz/175 g/1 cup pecans

method

1 Lightly grease a 9-inch/22-cm loose-bottom fluted tart pan. Sift the flour and salt into a food processor, add the butter, and process until the mixture resembles fine bread crumbs. Tip the mixture into a large bowl and add a little cold water, just enough to bring the dough together. Turn out on to a counter dusted with more flour and roll out the dough 3$^1/_4$ inches/ 8 cm larger than the pan. Carefully lift the dough into the pan and press to fit. Roll the rolling pin over the pan to neaten the edges and trim the excess dough. Fit a piece of parchment paper into the tart shell, fill with dried beans, and let chill in the refrigerator for 30 minutes.

2 Remove the shell from the refrigerator and bake in a preheated oven, 375°F/190°C, for 15 minutes, then remove the beans and paper and bake for an additional 10 minutes.

3 Empty the chestnut purée into a large bowl. Whip the cream until stiff and fold into the chestnut purée. Spoon into the cold tart shell and let chill for 2 hours. Melt the butter with the maple syrup and when bubbling add the pecans and stir for 1–2 minutes. Spoon on to parchment paper and let cool. When ready to serve, arrange the pecans on the chestnut cream.

chocolate fudge tart

ingredients

SERVES 6–8

flour, for sprinkling

12 oz/350 g ready-made
   unsweetened pie dough

confectioners' sugar, for dusting

filling

5 oz/140 g semisweet
   chocolate, finely chopped

6 oz/175 g butter, diced

12 oz/350 g/1³/₄ cups golden
   granulated sugar

3¹/₂ oz/100 g/³/₄ cup
   all-purpose flour

¹/₂ tsp vanilla extract

6 eggs, beaten

5 fl oz/150 ml/²/₃ cup
   whipped cream and
   ground cinnamon,
   to decorate

method

1 Roll out the pie dough on a lightly floured counter and use to line an 8-inch/20-cm deep loose-bottom tart pan. Prick the dough base lightly with a fork, then line with foil and fill with pie weights. Bake in a preheated oven, 400°F/200°C, for 12–15 minutes, or until the dough no longer looks raw. Remove the beans and foil and bake for 10 minutes more, or until the dough is firm. Let cool. Reduce the oven temperature to 350°F/180°C.

2 To make the filling, place the chocolate and butter in a heatproof bowl and melt over a pan of gently simmering water. Stir until smooth, then remove from the heat and let cool. Place the sugar, flour, vanilla extract, and eggs in a separate bowl and whisk until well blended. Stir in the butter and chocolate mixture.

3 Pour the filling into the tart shell and bake in the oven for 50 minutes, or until the filling is just set. Transfer to a wire rack to cool completely. Dust with confectioners' sugar before serving with whipped cream sprinkled lightly with cinnamon.

spiced baked goat yogurt

ingredients

SERVES 4

7 fl oz/200 ml goat yogurt

1/4 tsp ground mixed spice

1 tsp maple syrup

1/4 tsp vanilla extract

1/2 oz/15 g dried figs, very
    finely chopped

1 medium egg white

2 sliced fresh figs, 1/4 tsp
    maple syrup, and fresh
    mint leaves, to decorate

method

1 Mix the yogurt, mixed spice, maple syrup, vanilla extract, and dried figs together in a large bowl.

2 In a separate, very clean, greasefree bowl, lightly whisk the egg white until soft peaks form. Using a metal spoon, fold into the yogurt mixture. Spoon into 4 ramekins or a shallow, ovenproof dish.

3 Stand the ramekins or dish in a roasting pan and half-fill the pan with boiling water. Bake in a preheated oven, 275°F/140°C, for 15 minutes or until set.

4 Remove from the oven. To serve, lay the fresh fig slices on top of the set yogurts, drizzle with maple syrup, and decorate with fresh mint leaves.